Dr Snezhana Djambazova - Popordanoska, MD, PhD

ANOTHER WAY OF LIVING

A Journey to Infinite Peace, Immense Joy, and True Freedom

BOOK ONE

Third Revised and Expanded Edition

Dedication

Dedicated to the reader:

May love guide your steps,
and peace dwell in your heart.

May every challenge reveal your strength,
and every moment awaken your joy.

And may the Divinity within you shine so brightly
that it lights the way for others.

Note on the 3rd Edition

This is the third revised and expanded edition of *"Another Way of Living: A Journey to Infinite Peace, Immense Joy, and True Freedom,"* the first book in the *"Another Way of Living"* trilogy. In response to the growing interest and heartfelt feedback from many readers around the world, I expanded this edition to offer deeper exploration of each chapter, practical applications, and clinically proven strategies drawn from both my personal journey and my counselling practice. I have also refined and paraphrased parts of the text from the previous edition to ensure greater clarity and depth.

In addition to my own story, this book includes true stories from my counselling practice, shared to illustrate key insights and real-life transformations. To protect the confidentiality and privacy of my clients, all identifying details and names have been changed.

My intention is to provide you with even more practical tools, deep insights, and great inspiration to awaken your inner peace, and live in alignment with your highest self. Whether you are seeking clarity, joy, or true freedom, this edition is designed to guide you step by step towards a more meaningful, fulfilling, and empowered life.

Note: All reviews included in this book are quoted exactly as originally written. Variations in spelling reflect regional differences between British and American English.

Professional Editorial Review

"A thought-provoking roadmap to gratitude, self-knowledge, and inner peace, Another Way of Living (Book 1): A Journey to Infinite Peace, Immense Joy and True Freedom by Dr. Snezhana Djambazova-Popordanoska MD, PhD is an inspiring collection of holistic expertise. Focusing on practices that deliver meaningful change by harmonizing the physical, mental, and spiritual elements of everyday life, this book represents an all-encompassing path to wellness, focused on specific strategies to increase self-worth, manage stress, cultivate the mind-body connection, listen effectively, communicate compassionately, embrace self-love, and manage other daily pressures.

Presented in an original and memorable blend of poetry, philosophy, and science, this guide is more accessible than others in the field, displaying a unique vulnerability that is impactful in its openness, providing the necessary questions to shift one's outlook and behavior toward greater happiness and health."

- *"Self-Publishing Review,"*
Los Angeles, United States

Genuine Testimonials from Readers Worldwide

"Essential guidance for a real life full of joy, where freedom from our fears, limitations and false beliefs is the key for the only life we deserve. Strongly recommended."

\- Mido Ibrahim, Italy

"From the first page, I thought the author was talking directly to me. I could quickly identify the situations and found the solutions easy and simple."

\- Susan Saros, United States

"Customers should know that this book, "Another Way of Living," offers a plethora amount critical self-help and vital information to help guide the individual as well as to enlighten the individual of what to do and how to enhance his/her total wellness from a social, physical, emotional, intellectual, occupational, and spiritual perspective. The book

focuses on building resilience in these areas in order for the individual to find and maintain inner peace and to focus from a selflessness perspective by helping the individual recognize his/her 'selves' (self-love, self-care, self-acceptance, self-reliance, self-compassion, self-control, self-respect, and self-expression)."

\- Jocelyin Hardin, United States

"A great tool to help change your life. The book gives you tips on communication, self -care, understanding yourself and why we make the choices we do in our lives."

\- Louisa Mucciaccaro, Australia

"Discover a proven path to inner peace, confidence, and freedom from anxiety. Dr. Snezhana Djambazova-Popordanoska blends psychology, mindfulness, and spiritual insight into practical tools you can use daily. With short exercises for quick relief and deeper practices for lasting growth, this guide helps you stop overthinking, dissolve limiting beliefs, and build resilience, so peace and clarity become your natural state."

\- Austin Macdonald, United States

Acknowledgements

I am deeply grateful to my extraordinary husband, Emil, whose unwavering love, support, and faith in me have been a constant source of strength. His original profound and awakening poems have infused this book with depth, beauty and wisdom.

I am also profoundly grateful to:

- My wonderful children, Kristijan and Graciella, for their unwavering support, thoughtful ideas, and generous spirits.

- All my clients, whose inspiration and support played a vital role in bringing this book into being.

- All my relatives and friends, whose faith in my vision and loving encouragement continue to inspire me to share the path to peace, joy, and lasting happiness with others.

Contents

Author's Note

The following fascinating true story beautifully illustrates how the book *"Another Way of Living: A Journey to Infinite Peace, Immense Joy, and True* Freedom" was born. It began with a simple, ordinary day - one that unexpectedly opened the door to an extraordinary awakening.

My Story

It was a beautiful, sunny Sunday afternoon. It was the perfect time to play tennis with my family. As much as I wanted to spend some quality time with my husband and our children, while I was walking down to the tennis court, I couldn't stop thinking about all my work commitments waiting for me in the coming week.

On top of everything was my PhD thesis - three years of research and writing. *"When am I going to finish writing all these chapters? How can I balance my work, my thesis, and all my household duties?"* All these thoughts went around and around inside my head, creating a quiet inner storm. I was feeling overwhelmed with unpleasant feelings...

The tennis game started, but I wasn't really enjoying it. I wasn't truly present. My mind was overwhelmed with worries about my work, my thesis, my hectic schedule, and my lack of time to accomplish everything I wanted to achieve.

"This is too much for me," I was thinking. *"I have to become a superwoman to get everything done. When will I enjoy my life? Isn't life meant to be pleasurable?"* While being engaged in all these worrying thoughts, something completely unexpected happened - something that would change my life forever...

In the middle of the game, while running backwards to hit the tennis ball back to my husband, I lost my balance and fell hard, landing with my full body weight on my right hand. The next thing I remember was the pain - sharp, overwhelming, excruciating pain in my right hand. It was so severe that I couldn't stand up. I remained helplessly on the ground, unable to move.

My husband immediately ran over, and took me to the hospital. After taking the appropriate investigations, the doctor on duty approached me and said in an authoritative tone: *"You have a fracture in your right hand. This is a very rare type of fracture that takes a very long time to heal - if it heals at all. In ninety percent of cases, unfortunately, this kind of fracture does not heal spontaneously. Therefore, in such cases, the most common outcome is surgery. However, even after the operation, the prognosis is not good. In most cases patients experience permanent impairment in the use of the affected hand, leading to difficulties that can interfere with daily activities throughout their lifetime."*

"Is this really happening to me? This is my right hand - my dominant hand... How can I live like this?" All these thoughts went through my mind, but I wasn't able to say anything. I was in shock...

I left the hospital with a splint on my hand, and was instructed to wear it for two months. The doctor warned me that my hand needed complete rest during that time to allow the fracture to heal properly.

What followed felt like a waking nightmare. Suddenly, I couldn't do anything by myself. I needed help to get dressed, or to open the doors at home. I couldn't manage any of my usual domestic responsibilities, such as cooking, washing dishes, ironing, and so on. The only thing I could do - was to sit alone in silence, and reflect on my life...

I had so many questions racing through my mind, feeling confused, and miserable within. The main questions I asked myself were the following: *"Why has this happened to me? Is there something I need to change in my life?"* But no clear answers came - only the quiet, aching space that invited me to listen more deeply.

One day, my best friend came to visit me at home. I said to her, *"I've been contemplating my life, and I feel that something is not quite right. As I reflected on the way I've been living so far, I realised that I haven't truly been enjoying my life. I've been preoccupied with my work, my domestic responsibilities, my family, and my PhD thesis, neglecting all my other needs. I don't want to spend the rest of my life in pain, suffering, and misery. All I want is to be happy - to feel joyful and peaceful every single day. There must be another way of living. I need to change something - something that would bring more balance into my life. But... how can I do that?"*

My friend replied, *"I think that I know someone who can help you answer your questions. People go to him when they are searching for guidance or advice. His name is Cahil, and he is known as a spiritual teacher. People say that you always feel peace, serenity, and joy in his presence."*

When I finally met Cahil, I could hardly believe my eyes. This man radiated immense peace, joy and love in every gesture, in every glance. His presence was simply inspiring… I thought to myself, *"Perhaps Cahil will teach me how to be happier, how to create a more balanced life. He can be my guru."*

My wish soon became a reality. Following Cahil's guidance, I decided to make meaningful changes in my life. I embraced a holistic approach to my health and wellbeing - one that nurtured my body, mind, and spirit. Gradually, I began to notice subtle yet profound shifts in my daily experiences - the way I thought, moved, and connected with myself and the world around me. This new way of living, grounded in balance and harmony across the mental, physical, and spiritual dimensions of myself, has transformed my life.

The seeds of faith, perseverance, and self-belief I had planted within me began to blossom into tangible blessings. Six months after my fracture, I visited my doctor again. After conducting the necessary investigations, he looked at me and said, *"I can't explain scientifically what really happened, but your hand has healed completely. This is a miracle! Good luck in your new life."*

From my guru I learned that there truly is another way of living - another way of being. By embracing this path, I began to experience deep inner peace, joy, and serenity every day, and to radiate it outward. I discovered how to create poetry in my life, transforming each moment into joy, celebration, and laughter. I learned what it means to be fully alive. This is true life.

I expressed my heartfelt gratitude to my spiritual teacher and promised him that I would share this wisdom and practical skills I learned from him with as many people as possible. And that is exactly what I did. My vision became a reality, and my new organisation, *Another Way Life Education,* was born. I began working as a counsellor, mindfulness coach, and motivational speaker. I also wrote the self-help trilogy, *"Another Way of Living,"* which has reached readers worldwide and transformed countless lives. Through my counselling and coaching sessions - both in person and online - I have helped thousands of individuals worldwide transform their lives into ones filled with enduring peace, joy, and love.

For more information about my work, please visit: **www.anotherwayeducation.org**

About This Book

This book invites you to explore life's most significant questions: how to rise above fear, experience lasting peace, and rediscover your true worth. It then gently leads you towards the deeper questions of existence - how to find meaning in life and reach self-realisation - questions that, when left unexamined, often lie at the root of human suffering.

Drawing upon clinically proven strategies and inspiring real-life transformations from my counselling practice, this book offers a gentle step-by-step journey of healing and awakening. It is a guide to emotional freedom, inner peace, and the realisation of your highest self - a journey towards living each moment with love, serenity, and divine purpose.

As you turn each page, may you find insights that awaken your heart and light your path. May these words inspire you to discover the limitless peace, joy, and wisdom within you - and guide you towards becoming the highest, most radiant, and most authentic version of yourself.

With love,

Snezhana Djambazova-Popordanoska

Enjoying Life Fully

Q: How can we enjoy our life fully and experience joy daily?

A: The ultimate goal in life is to be content within, and to experience inner peace, immense joy and lasting happiness on a consistent basis. Hence, to enjoy your life fully, you need to identify your needs in the present moment, and aim to meet those needs as soon as you become aware of them. Remember, your immediate needs are your priority, and your main task is to fulfil them.

If you don't act on your needs in the present moment, you'll frequently experience feelings of dissatisfaction and frustration. These negative feelings inside you can resurface at any moment when you are in close contact with the people around you, transferring your negative energy to them. This in turn, can cause relationship problems, conflicts, and feelings of disconnection from others. Over time, this negative energy will build up in your body, interfering with the functioning of the organs of your body as well as your emotional wellbeing. Therefore, if not disposed of properly, this negative energy may eventually cause development of a physical or mental illness, an accident, or even an injury.

One of my clients, Sarah, vividly illustrated this. Sarah was a 38-year-old journalist who prided herself on being reliable and supportive. She would often say "yes" to every request at work - covering for her colleagues, taking on extra projects, and staying late to meet her deadlines. Skipping lunches became her norm, and she convinced herself that she was simply being efficient.

At first, she brushed off the signs of strain, telling herself that she was just "a little tired." But over time, Sarah began to feel a gnawing sense of emptiness, as though no matter how much she gave, it was never enough. The more she ignored her needs and feelings, the more resentment quietly built within her. She began waking up with tension headaches and a heavy feeling in her chest. Yet she kept pushing through, afraid of letting anyone down.

Her emotional state also shifted. Small frustrations at work triggered sharp reactions, and she found herself snapping at her colleagues that she genuinely cared about. Sarah later admitted in counselling that what hurt her most was not the headaches or the exhaustion, but the guilt and shame she felt after those outbursts. She described feeling "trapped" - on the outside appearing capable and strong, but inside carrying a growing storm of fatigue, frustration, and self-blame. Eventually, her body forced her to stop. The headaches worsened, her energy plummeted, and she was signed off on extended sick leave.

In our sessions, Sarah realised that her body had been signalling distress for months, but because she ignored her needs for rest, nourishment, and maintaining healthy boundaries, the cost became far greater, affecting not only her health, but also her relationships and her sense of self-worth.

Sarah's experience is a clear reminder that when we neglect our needs, life itself finds a way to draw our attention back to them - often through discomfort, fatigue, or emotional pain. That's why it is worth reflecting on your way of living.

To begin this process, you may gently reflect on the following questions:

- *"Who knows best what my needs are at any given moment?"*
- *"Whose responsibility is to meet my needs?"*
- *"Who is creating my day?"*

The answer is always the same - you. No one can know better than you what your immediate needs are and how to fulfil them. Only you can create your day. Only you can design your life. Only you can write your own destiny!

To enjoy every single moment of your life, it is vital to remain fully aware of your needs in each moment. The better you are at identifying and satisfying your immediate needs, the more content you will feel. Hence, as often as possible, during the day, focus your full attention on yourself. And after that peaceful period of a few moments, ask yourself, *"What do I really need now?"* This simple yet powerful question centres you in the present moment and redirects your attention inward.

The impact of this practice becomes clear when we look at real-life experiences. Take, for example, my client Daniel, a 34-year-old police officer. He often felt resentful that his partner wasn't giving him enough attention. Daniel longed for closeness but didn't realise that his sense of emptiness came from his unmet needs, not from his partner's actions.

During our counselling sessions, Daniel learned to pause and check in with himself - a practice he began applying throughout his day to recognise what he truly needed in each moment. Sometimes, he discovered he was simply tired and needed rest; other times, he needed connection, inspiration, or movement. By taking small actions every day - calling a friend, listening to music, going for a jog, or journaling his thoughts - he began meeting his own needs instead of expecting others to fulfil them. Gradually, Daniel became more balanced, less reactive, and more at peace. His relationship with his partner naturally deepened as a result of his newfound self-awareness.

Daniel's experience illustrates a universal truth: when we take responsibility for our own needs, we empower ourselves and free others from the burden of making us happy.

To understand this process more deeply, it is helpful to become familiar with our core human needs - the essential areas of our Being that continuously seek balance and nourishment.

Core Human Needs

Throughout the day, you might have different unfulfilled needs. For example, your need at any given moment might be one of the following:

- **Physical needs:** hunger, thirst, physical activity, rest or massage.

  After a long morning of online meetings, you notice you feel sluggish. Instead of grabbing another coffee, you step outside for a 15-minute walk. The fresh air and body movement can refresh both your body and your mind and uplift your spirits.

- **Mental needs:** reading, writing, drawing, painting, or playing music.

  If you notice that your thoughts are becoming dull or restless, you might need some intellectual stimulation. Activities such as reading a few pages of an inspiring book, journaling, sketching, or playing music can nourish your mind and bring you greater clarity.

- **Spiritual needs:** spending time alone in silence, connecting with nature, having a spiritual conversation with a friend, listening to relaxing music, or practising yoga, or meditation.

  When you feel disconnected or lost, take a few minutes to sit in silence, meditate, practise yoga, or simply watch the sunset. These moments of stillness will allow your inner wisdom to surface and will bring you peace within.

- **Social needs:** spending quality time with your beloved, going out and meeting new people, or having a coffee with a friend.

  Sometimes what you truly need is human warmth – a friendly chat, a shared laugh, or a comforting hug. Reaching out to your loved one, joining a group activity, or having a coffee with your friend can instantly uplift your mood and restore a sense of connection.

Remember, when you learn to recognise and address your needs as they arise, its fulfilment will bring you immediate satisfaction. In this way, you will learn to live in the present, embracing life as it unfolds, and enjoying each moment more deeply.

Reflection & Practice: Connecting with Your Needs

Try these simple prompts and exercises to help you apply the ideas from this chapter:

Daily Check-In

- Pause at least three times today and ask yourself: *"What do I really need right now?"*

- Optionally, you may write down your answers to increase your self- awareness.

Need Awareness Journal

- Each evening, reflect on the moments you honoured your needs and the times you ignored them.

- Ask yourself: *"How did I feel in each case?"*

Body - Mind - Spirit - Social Balance

- Draw a circle and divide it into four quadrants: Body, Mind, Spirit, Social.

- Write one small action you can take tomorrow for each area to nurture balance throughout the day.

Reframe Responsibility

- Journal about: *"How does my life shift when I take full responsibility for meeting my needs?"*

Gratitude in Action

- Each time you meet an immediate need, pause and say silently: *"Thank you for taking care of me."*

Remember that your immediate needs are your true priority in life. They are the voice of your body, mind, and soul calling you back to balance. By regularly honouring your needs -s whether for rest, nourishment, connection, or quiet - you affirm your worthiness.

When you listen and respond to your needs at any given moment, you reclaim your inner power. You remind yourself that you deserve care, love, and attention just as much as anyone else. This simple act of self-care will fill your heart with joy, restore your energy, and ground you in the vibrant flow of life. From this place of wholeness, your choices will become clearer, your relationships more authentic, and your journey more purposeful.

Achieving a Peaceful State of Mind

"Nobody can bring you peace but yourself."
- Ralph Waldo Emerson

Q: How can I stop being unceasingly active throughout the day and begin to feel more calm and peaceful?

A: First you need to ask yourself the following question: *"Why am I constantly active throughout the day?"* To answer this question, it is important to understand that whenever the human mind is dissatisfied, it will constantly seek to be engaged in any kind of activity. You may not even realise it, but this busyness acts as a distraction – a way to escape from your inner discomfort, unresolved problems, or unpleasant emotions. Therefore, whenever you feel restless or unhappy inside yourself, you will always have an ardent desire to be involved in any activity, regardless of the demands of the situation, or your actual needs.

Instead of being constantly active, you need to learn how to respond to the situations in life in a calm and peaceful manner. It is important to note here that there is a difference between feeling the urge to be constantly involved in any kind of activity and responding calmly to the demands of a situation. The difference is that the urge to be busy all the time arises from a restless and discontented mind, whereas spontaneous action emerges from a peaceful state of mind. Hence, to cultivate a more peaceful state of mind, you must increase your self-awareness.

Here are some useful ways to boost your self-awareness in everyday life:

Step 1: Observe Yourself

Start by observing yourself throughout the day without any judgement. As you become engaged in any kind of activity, you may ask yourself:

- *"What is the purpose of this activity?"*
- *"Do I truly want to do this now, or am I avoiding something unpleasant inside myself?"*

- *"Am I enjoying this, or is it purely out of habit?"*

For example, you might find yourself scrolling through social media repeatedly. Instead, you may pause for a moment, and gently ask yourself: *"Am I doing this to connect and relax, or am I avoiding an uncomfortable feeling within me, like boredom or anxiety?"* As you answer these questions, notice your feelings and bodily sensations.

If you identify any unpleasant feelings or uncomfortable physical sensations in yourself, this might mean that you have satisfied the need to be engaged in that particular activity. When you arrive at this moment, you need to stop for a few moments, and do nothing but enjoy your own presence. In this way, you will connect with your inner centre – the peaceful essence of your existence. Then, from this state of mental stillness you can focus all your attention and energy on the next activity that needs to be done.

Step 2: Practise Small Pauses

Instead of jumping immediately from one task to the next, practise inserting intentional pauses between your daily activities. Even 30 seconds of mindful presence can help you reset your mind. For instance, before sending an email, take a moment to breathe and focus on your intention. Before starting your commute, simply feel your feet on the ground and observe your surroundings. Over time, these micro-pauses will create a sense of inner spaciousness and calm throughout your day.

Step 3: Do Nothing, Really

It may feel uncomfortable at first, but deliberately doing nothing is one of the most powerful ways to reconnect with your inner peace. Sit quietly, and simply be present. If any thoughts arise, simply observe them without engaging. If you do this frequently, gradually, you will notice a sense of calmness that stays with you even after this practice.

Step 4: Bring Joy in Each Action

When you are connected to your inner calm, you will approach each task with greater clarity and presence. So, before engaging in any activity, pause and ask yourself: *"Does this activity bring me joy? Is it meaningful to me?"* Acting from this centered state of mind will help you to use your energy efficiently, and engage fully in whatever you do.

Rather than moving through your chores automatically, give each task your conscious attention – whether it is washing dishes, responding to messages, or completing work assignments. Importantly, as you do this, notice your physical sensations, and the sense of satisfaction that comes from completing each task with intention and joy. Then, even the simplest activities will become moments of presence, fulfillment, and quite delight.

Here are some practical ways to cultivate joy in your daily activities:

- **Bring mindfulness into each task:** Notice the textures, sounds, smells, or sensations involved. For example, feel the warmth of the water, and the smoothness of the dishes while washing them.

- **Add small moments of gratitude:** Appreciate the opportunity to take care of your home, body, or work. Gratitude can transform even simple tasks into sources of joy.

- **Create a pleasant environment:** Play your favourite music, open a window, light a scented candle, or surround yourself with colours or objects that uplift you.

- **Infuse playfulness:** Approach your tasks with a light, curious, or playful attitude. Can folding laundry feel like a rhythm or dance? Can replying to emails become a game of clarity and efficiency?

- **Focus on purpose:** Remind yourself how even small tasks, like making dinner for your family - can contribute to your wellbeing and the wellbeing of your beloved. Connecting your actions to a bigger purpose can make them feel meaningful and rewarding.

- **Celebrate completion:** Pause for a brief moment to notice your accomplishment before moving to the next task. A small acknowledgement of your efforts will bring more joy into your life.

By approaching each action in this way, even everyday routines can become opportunities to cultivate more presence, satisfaction, and joy. Over time, this approach will transform your daily routine into a richer, more vibrant experience of life.

Step 5: Make Peace a Daily Habit

- Start and end your day with a 5-minute mindfulness ritual.

- Engage in calming activities like mindful walking, journaling, or gentle stretching.
- Remind yourself frequently: *"I choose peace in this moment."*

The more frequently you practise this relaxed state of mind between your daily activities, the more mental energy you will preserve. This energy can then be channelled into purposeful, creative, and fulfilling action. This in turn, will enhance not only your productivity but also your overall wellbeing. Remember that each time you practise this, you are nurturing a life of purpose, joy, and harmony – reminding yourself that the power to transform your life is always in your hands, here and now.

Overcoming Suffering

"We need to be aware of the suffering, but retain our clarity, calmness and strength so we can help transform the situation."
- Thich Nhat Hanh

Q: Is suffering a necessary requirement for happiness?

A: To answer this question, first, you need to understand the real cause of suffering. Suffering is always the result of not accepting the present moment as it is – of not accepting your current life situation. It is the refusal of any unpleasant emotions. It is the denial of life and the natural laws that govern it. Suffering is an indication that you are resisting the reality.

It is important to understand that suffering is not a prerequisite for happiness. Suffering is a fruit of distorted thinking that is not attuned to the reality. Happiness, by contrast, is a result of an enlightened mind that can clearly see the reality. In fact, both suffering and happiness are interpretations of the reality, of how you look at it. So, in essence, you are the creator of your own suffering, as well as the creator of your own happiness.

Each of us can overcome suffering, and achieve a lasting state of tranquility and joy, if we are willing to raise our awareness, and expand our consciousness. The important question is this: *"Do you want to escape from suffering temporarily, or do you want to be free from it entirely?"* Temporary escapes – through alcohol, medications, endless entertainment, or intellectual justifications – may numb your pain briefly, but they come with the inevitable consequences of dependence, regret, and emptiness. But if you really want to be free from suffering, you must stop running away from it and become aware of it. You need to accept your suffering without any judgement. This simple yet profound act opens the doorway to true freedom. In that still moment of acceptance, you begin to see that your pain is not your enemy – it is your teacher, guiding you towards truth. It reveals a simple yet powerful lesson: peace does not come from escape, but from acceptance.

Accept What Is, Transform What You Can

One of the deepest sources of suffering in life is our struggle against reality itself. We wish things were different, replay our mistakes, cling to regret, and try to rewrite what has already been written. In doing so, we exhaust our spirit and lose touch with the peace that is always available in the present moment. But healing begins the moment we stop resisting what is. When we stop fighting life and start flowing with it, something within us softens – and in that stillness, wisdom arises. As the timeless Serenity Prayer reminds us:

"Grant me the serenity to accept the things I cannot change, courage to change the things I can, and wisdom to know the difference."

These words hold the essence of conscious living. Acceptance is not about giving up or becoming passive – it is about finding peace with the truth of the moment before deciding how to respond. It is the courageous act of making peace with this moment – of saying, *"This is what is,"* before deciding, *"Now, what will I do?"* When you fight against what has already happened, you lose your power. When you accept it, you reclaim your energy, your clarity, and your peace. When you make peace with what is, you free the energy that was once trapped in resistance and redirect it towards what truly matters.

Acceptance doesn't mean tolerating injustice or enduring toxicity. It means letting go of the illusion that the past could be different or that you can control every outcome. Instead, pause and ask yourself with honesty and compassion: *"Can I change this?"*

If the answer is "yes" – act, with clarity, kindness, and strength. If the answer is "no" – breathe deeply, let go, and trust the unfolding of life. True acceptance doesn't mean agreeing with everything; it means aligning with reality so that your next step springs from wisdom, not fear. From that still, quiet centre within – wise, conscious, and purposeful action flows naturally.

When you live this way, you stop being a victim of circumstances. You stop spinning in loops of fear, guilt, or regret. You begin to move through life not with tension, but with peace. Because peace isn't the absence of problems – it's the presence of clarity and grace within them. So, when life feels heavy, whisper to your heart: *"I will accept what is, and change what I can."* In that simple truth lies the beginning of freedom -and the quiet revolution that changes everything.

To see this principle in action, let's consider Angela's experience in her workplace. Angela, a 42-year-old accountant, came to counselling utterly exhausted and quietly bitter. Each morning, before even getting out of bed, she would feel a heavy knot in her stomach. The thought of returning to the office filled her with dread. She believed that her efforts at work went unnoticed by her manager and her colleagues, that no one truly appreciated how much she cared, and how much she tried to do things right.

In reality, it wasn't the office itself that was crushing her spirit – it was the silent war she was fighting in her own mind. Her resistance to what was – her constant "shoulds" and "if onlys" – kept her trapped in a cycle of pain and suffering. The more she tried to mentally escape her situation, the more miserable she became.

In our counselling sessions, Angela began to see this clearly. At first, she resisted even that insight – *"So, you're saying this is all my fault?"* she asked tearfully one day. But slowly, she came to understand that accepting reality didn't mean approving of it. It meant freeing herself from the emotional chains of resistance.

Every morning, she started a new practice. As she opened her eyes, instead of thinking about everything that might go wrong, she whispered to herself:

"My workplace may not be perfect, but for now, this is where I am. I am grateful for the income that supports me and my loved ones, and for the opportunities here to learn and grow. I will give my best to this company and contribute with integrity, making a positive difference in my clients' lives whenever I can."

At first, these words felt mechanical, almost forced. But within a few weeks, she noticed something subtle shifting. The knot in her stomach loosened. The familiar sense of dread began to fade. She still saw her manager's flaws and her colleagues' shortcomings, but they no longer dominated her thoughts. She began to notice small moments of goodness – a client's appreciation, a shared laugh in the lunchroom, a quiet sense of satisfaction after finishing a project well.

By accepting her reality rather than resisting it, Angela found an unexpected sense of inner peace. She decided to focus on the parts of her work that genuinely brought her joy – helping her clients, solving complex financial problems, and feeling competent in her craft.

Gradually, she let go of the need to control her manager's actions or her colleagues' behaviours. Within months, her stress eased, her sleep improved, and she rediscovered small pleasures she had long forgotten – the warmth of the morning sun on her face, the calm rhythm of her breathing, the laughter of her children when she returned home.

Angela's story is a gentle reminder that when we stop fighting against life as it is, and begin to meet it with openness and acceptance, suffering loses its power over us. The mind softens, the heart heals, and the inner peace – which has always been within us – begins to flow naturally again. Angela's story is just one example of how shifting from resistance to acceptance can transform everyday suffering.

Now, let's explore how you can begin practising this in your own life.

Reflection Exercise: Transforming Resistance into Acceptance

1. Identify one area of your work, personal life or daily routine where you feel the most resistance.

2. Ask yourself: *"What would it look like if I fully accepted this situation as it is?"*

3. Journal your thoughts about how your life might shift if you focused your energy on what is within your control rather than what is not.

Remember that acceptance helps to overcome suffering! Yet deeper freedom comes when we also practise detachment from people, outcomes, and expectations.

Detachment: Transforming Attachment into Freedom

Suffering may also arise when you cling tightly - whether to your emotions, to others' opinions, or to the way you think life should be. This clinging, or attachment, makes you vulnerable to every insult, every criticism and every disappointment. Detachment, on the other hand, is the ability to remain rooted in peace, even when life shakes you.

Being detached doesn't mean being indifferent – it means that you can care deeply for yourself and others while protecting your inner world from being controlled by others' reactions.

The following principles may help you transform suffering into strength by loosening attachment, and embracing detachment in your daily life:

1. Turn Insults into Opportunities for Growth

When someone insults you, it often reflects their own inner turmoil, not your value. If you take it personally, you may become attached to their negativity, and then, you may suffer. But if you see it as a lesson, the insult may become an opportunity for you to grow in patience, compassion, and resilience.

A powerful example of this principle comes from one of my clients, Lydia, a 47-year-old retail manager, who often felt undermined and dismissed by her younger colleagues. They frequently mocked her for being "old-fashioned" in her work style, making comments about her methods, her appearance, and even her pace. At first, Lydia felt a mix of frustration, embarrassment, and self-doubt. She often questioned herself: *"Am I out of touch? Do they think I'm incompetent?"* Her initial reaction was defensive; she tried to justify her decisions and correct them in front of the entire team. Unfortunately, this only fuelled more tension, and the mocking sometimes became sharper, leaving her feeling drained and anxious at work.

In our counselling sessions, Lydia explored her feelings of vulnerability, and recognised that her energy was being hijacked by their words. She began practising detachment – not indifference, but the ability to observe her colleagues' insults without letting them define her self-worth or dictate her responses. Instead of arguing or trying to prove herself, she started to respond with calm authority and quiet compassion, or simply allowing silence to speak for her confidence. When one of her colleagues teased her about being "slow," she smiled gently and said: *"Perhaps that's because I like to take the time to do things properly – it saves everyone effort in the end."* When another made a sarcastic remark about her "old-fashioned" approach, she replied warmly, *"Maybe. But kindness and patience never really go out of style, do they?"* Her tone was light, but her words carried quiet wisdom. She wasn't trying to win or correct – only to stay true to herself and her values.

There were moments when she sensed that words would only deepen the tension, and in those moments, she chose silence – a calm, grounded silence that carried neither resentment nor submission. She met their remarks with understanding, seeing their behaviour as a reflection of their own insecurity rather than a judgement of her worth. Her stillness became her strength, and her gentle presence began to change the emotional atmosphere around her.

Over time, her colleagues' reactions shifted. They noticed that Lydia no longer reacted with defensiveness or irritation. Some initially continued to test her boundaries, but gradually, the disrespect faded. Her composed and measured responses earned quiet respect, and she noticed a subtle change in the team dynamic: their collaboration improved, and the mocking ceased altogether.

By detaching from the sting of the insult, Lydia reclaimed her confidence and presence. She began to trust her judgement and leadership style again, and this steadiness was eventually recognised by senior management – leading to her promotion. Through this experience, Lydia not only strengthened her professional authority but also discovered the profound personal freedom that comes from letting go of her reactive impulses and holding her own emotional ground.

Reflection Question: The next time someone insults you, instead of reacting, ask yourself: *"How can I respond in a calm, confident and respectful manner to this person by keeping my inner peace?"*

2. Don't Let Other People's Words Dictate Your Emotions

Your emotions are your responsibility. Allowing someone's criticism or praise to control your self-worth may rob you of your freedom. Detachment here means to remember the following: *"People's words are just their subjective opinions based on their own personal perspectives. Their words reflect themselves, not me."*

For example, Samuel, a 29-year-old software engineer, was deeply affected by his boss's criticism. A single negative comment could ruin his entire week. Through counselling, he learned to separate constructive feedback from emotional triggers. He began to ask himself, *"Is this feedback really useful for me, or is it just my boss's frustration?"* This detachment gave him freedom. He stopped measuring his value by his boss's mood and started focusing on his own standards of excellence.

Reflection Exercise: Write down the last critical remark that hurt you. Ask yourself: *"Is this really about me, or is it a reflection of their own struggles? Is this situation about my actions, or is it about their own feelings and judgements?"*

3. See Every Interaction as a Learning Experience

Every encounter - pleasant or unpleasant - can be a powerful teacher. If someone is rude - it may be an opportunity to practise patience and compassion. If someone is kind - it may be an opportunity to practise gratitude. Remember that when you shift your perspective, no interaction is wasted! Every interaction, no matter how unpleasant, can teach you something valuable.

Tom's experience illustrates how adopting a mindset of learning and growing can turn irritation into wisdom. At 61, he drove a taxi and often faced rude customers. He used to go home bitter and angry. Through counselling, he adopted a new perspective: *"Each passenger is my teacher."* When some passenger was unkind, he practised compassion: *"Perhaps they are in pain."* When someone was joyful, he let himself be uplifted. By detaching from judgement, and embracing a loving and compassionate attitude, Tom turned his daily frustrations into a source of wisdom and joy.

Reflection Exercise: At the end of the day, write down one thing you learned from a challenging interaction. Also, recall one moment when you were loving, kind, or compassionate towards yourself or someone else, and note how it made you feel. Practising this regularly helps you cultivate awareness, empathy, and a sense of growth, turning everyday challenges into opportunities for peace and wisdom.

Remember, true transformation begins with acceptance. Acceptance is the gateway to peace. When you allow reality to be as it is, the grip of suffering eases, and a quite calm returns to your heart. Through detachment, you can fully engage with life without clinging - by turning insults into opportunities, criticism into strength, and intense emotions into passing waves. By embracing what is, and transforming what you can, you liberate yourself. You awaken to your truest self - a self that is untouched by chaos or fear - and step into a life guided by grace, peace, and freedom.

Overcoming Fear

Q: How can we overcome, or at least reduce our everyday fears?

A: Fear is a poison that contaminates the subconscious mind, which in turn can completely destroy the willpower of the conscious mind. When fearful thoughts and corresponding feelings occur, the brain discharges the message of fear and threat to all organs in the body. Fear paralyses the heart, weakens the immune system, disturbs the digestive system's function, and causes many other disturbances in our body. It intensifies and magnifies our physical pain and suffering. Fear has detrimental impact not only on our physical health, but also on our mental health, debilitating our motivation, courage, and willpower.

Fear as a Magnet

Fear produces a toxic magnetism which draws to itself the objects of fear, just as a magnet draws to itself pieces of iron. Therefore, you do not need to fear accidents, unpleasant situations, or diseases - if you have had them in the past. Rather, be afraid of fear itself, for fear may bring repeated accidents, undesirable situations, and illnesses to you. Hence, your work is to drive out your self-imposed enemies - your fears from your mind.

It is important to note here that many people, for example, live with the fear of illness. After a health scare, the mind can become hyper-vigilant, misinterpreting every small sensation as a sign of danger. Ordinary sensations - a fleeting ache, a slight cough, or a moment of fatigue - can be misinterpreted as a signal that the illness is returning. Over time, this pattern of thinking can become automatic, creating a constant state of tension and worry that is exhausting both mentally and physically.

The story of Michael, a 55-year-old electrician, vividly illustrates this phenomenon. After recovering from a severe bout of pneumonia, Michael found himself trapped in a cycle of health anxiety. Every cough or minor discomfort triggered intense fear that the illness would return. His thoughts became dominated by "what if" scenarios, and the anxiety began to amplify physical symptoms such as shortness of breath and heart palpitations. This constant state of fear not only worsened his health concerns but also gradually eroded his enjoyment of everyday life - activities he had once loved - like walking in the park or socialising with his friends, now felt overshadowed by fear and worry.

In therapy, Michael learned to see his anxiety as an exaggerated response, not as a prediction. Through regular practice of cognitive and relaxation techniques, he learned to shift his mindset - from the limiting belief, *"I am fragile and always at risk of getting sick,"* to a more empowering one, *"My body is strong, resilient, and capable of healing."* This practice helped him to confidently embrace his health and wellbeing once again.

Michael's journey reminds us that often, fear is not a reflection of reality itself but a fearful story the mind creates. When we learn to question that story, and replace it with a truth that empowers us, we can reclaim both our peace and our strength.

Tracing Fear to Its Root

When someone is filled with fear, they not only feel it within themselves but also project it onto their surroundings. Through the lens of fear, the world appears hostile, full of threats and dangers. Fear is a negative, destructive energy which disconnects, contracts, destroys, and harms... It blurs the vision, and it is a cause of poor decisions and wrong actions that eventually lead to failure and suffering.

Fear ordinarily produces negative outcomes. For example, fear of losing a relationship can create jealousy. Jealousy, in turn, can lead to lying, manipulation, or even violence. Similarly, fear of scarcity may produce greed, which can manifest as competitiveness, impatience, or selfishness. When energy leaves you in fear, it will bring only discomfort or pain in your body. If you choose to live with fear, jealousy, or greed, you will learn your lessons in life through pain, suffering, and a sense of loss.

I witnessed this pattern in Anna, a 32-year-old hairdresser, whose deeply ingrained fear created ongoing conflict in her marriage. Her deep fear of being abandoned caused her to frequently check her husband's phone, question his every move, and even lie to "test" his loyalty. This created tension and mistrust in their relationship. Once Anna realised that her feeling of jealousy came from an old childhood wound - her father leaving the family when she was six, she began working on replacing the negative belief: *"Everyone I love will leave me,"* with a healthy one: *"I am worthy of love, respect and security."* Over time, her fear loosened its grip, and the relationship with her husband became more trusting.

Anna's journey shows us that fear often disguises itself as jealousy, control or mistrust - but at its core, it is usually a wound from the past that hasn't been healed. The turning point comes when we recognise the source of our fear and challenge the beliefs that keep it alive. True freedom begins the moment we stop letting yesterday's pain dictate today's relationships. When we gently shift our fear-based beliefs into ones rooted in self-worth, trust, and security, we free ourselves from the weight of the past. Then, we can embrace love with greater openness and live with a heart that feels safe and strong.

Yet Anna's story is just one example. Fear is not only personal - it is universal. Across cultures and centuries, humans have grappled with fear, noticing how it shapes their thoughts, decisions, and actions. This leads us to a deeper understanding - much of what we experience as fear is not reality itself, but a projection of the mind.

The Illusion of Fear

Now, imagine living without that heavy weight of fear pressing on your chest each morning. Picture yourself moving through life with calm clarity, a steady mind, and a courageous heart. Obstacles no longer feel like traps, but invitations to grow. This is not just a dream - it can be your reality. For over 2,500 years, Buddhist wisdom has guided people to see that much of what we call fear is only an illusion.

Buddha taught that fear is rarely about the present reality - it is usually a story the mind creates about the future. Think of standing on the edge of a cliff: your heart races, your palms sweat, and your stomach tightens. But are you actually falling? Are you really in danger right now? No. The mind simply projects an imagined catastrophe. Remember, fear is not a fact - it is simply a thought.

It is important to understand that most of our fears are not innate - they are learned from others along the way. We were not born with them, except for two natural fears: the fear of falling and the fear of loud noises. When we begin to see fear as a habit of the mind rather than a reflection of reality, its power starts to dissolve. This is explored more deeply in the chapter *"Fear and Release from It"* in my self-help book *"Another Way of Living: How to Dissolve the Ego and Realise Your Divine Potential"*- the third book in my trilogy.

Fear is like a shadow - when you turn away, it looms large, but when you face it directly, it dissolves. As Robin Sharma wisely observed, *"Most fears are nothing more than illusions. And yet they rule our lives."* So, to overcome fear, you must take courage to face it directly and perceive any unpleasant or unpredictable situations in life without any judgement. Non-judgemental awareness dissolves fear, allowing acceptance and inner calm to arise. When you see fear as an illusion, fear loses its control. Then, you will no longer let it dictate your choices and decisions in life. Instead, you will move with courage, resilience and grace, open to new possibilities.

From Fear to Freedom

Now that you understand that fear is a habit of the mind rather than an absolute truth, you can begin to take practical steps to free yourself from its grip. Recognising fear as an illusion is powerful - but awareness alone is not always enough. To truly transform fear, you must also engage with it, question it, and replace its negative and limiting thoughts with more balanced and empowering ones.

Remember, fear often grows when you allow your thoughts to run unchecked. In other words, fear is an emotional state resulting from errors in your thinking - a product of unrealistic judgements and distorted perceptions of your undesirable life's situations. When you begin to see fear as a mental habit rather than as an absolute truth, you create space for freedom, and change.

One of my clients, Sophia, a 27-year-old marketing executive, experienced this firsthand. She would feel a knot of panic in her stomach and an almost paralysing tightness in her chest at the mere thought of speaking in front of others. Even small team meetings caused her sleepless nights and a constant loop of "what if" assumptions racing through her mind. In our counselling sessions, Sophia gradually uncovered the negative thoughts driving this fear: *"If I speak in front of others, I'll embarrass myself."*

Like many of us, Sophia's fear did not come from the present moment. It was not that she was in immediate danger or that something terrible was actually about to happen - it was her unexamined, fearful thoughts, magnifying imagined threats. She imagined forgetting her words, tripping over her sentences, or seeing judgemental looks on her colleagues' faces. Each mental image created real physical sensations of anxiety: her heart would race, her hands would tremble, and her breathing would become shallow.

This fear began to shape her behaviour as well. Sophia found herself avoiding opportunities to speak, rehearsing endlessly in private, and feeling embarrassed about even small presentations at work. Ironically, her avoidance reinforced her anxiety - she never gave herself the chance to experience success, and the cycle of fear continued. She was the prisoner of her fear.

Through reflection and gentle questioning in our counselling sessions, Sophia began to see how her assumptions based on fear were patterns she had learned, rather than facts. Recognising that her fear was arising from her mind's projections rather than the reality of the situation, became her first step towards reclaiming control. She began to understand that her anxiety could be challenged, not by forcing herself to ignore it, but by consciously examining it and transforming her responses.

To help Sophia move beyond this paralysing fear, I introduced a practical cognitive tool, called *"Challenging Negative Thoughts."* Rooted in Cognitive Behavioural Therapy, this clinically proven method helps to bring fearful thoughts into the light of awareness and gently dismantle them by guiding you through a series of structured questions. Over the years, this incredibly helpful took has supported thousands of my clients worldwide in transforming their fears and anxiety into calm, confidence, and clarity.

Let's walk through this tool step by step, using Sophia's own experience to illustrate how it can be applied to overcome fear in real-life situations, such as public speaking. Here's how it works in practice.

Challenging Negative Thoughts

Step 1: *What exactly am I worried/upset/ anxious about?*

Sophia wrote down her recurring thought that made her anxious: *"If I speak in front of others,*

I'll embarrass myself and everyone will laugh at me." By putting her fear into words, she began the process of observing it, rather than being consumed by it.

Step 2: *What is the worst outcome that can happen in this situation?*

She imagined the worst-case scenario: *"I might freeze, forget what to say, and my colleagues will think I am incapable and unprofessional."*

Step 3: *How likely is the worst possible scenario going to happen (on a scale of 0 to 100%)?*

At first, Sophia rated it as 70%. But when she reflected, she realised that she had never actually frozen completely in a meeting before, and her colleagues were generally supportive. Her percentage dropped to about 30%.

Step 4: *What is the evidence that the worst possible outcome is going to happen?*

This question proved to be a turning point for Sophia. As she reflected, she realised there was no concrete evidence that her fear would actually come true - only the anxious story that her mind had been telling itself. Her worry was rooted in her unexamined fearful assumptions, not facts.

(She then took a few slow, calming breaths, allowing herself a moment of clarity before moving on to the next steps.)

Step 5: *What can be the best outcome in this situation? What do I really want to happen?*

Sophia wrote: *"I'll present my ideas clearly, be calm and confident, and gain my team's respect. They'll listen attentively and value my contribution."*

Step 6: *What can I do to attract the best possible outcome?*

She decided to prepare her slides thoroughly, practise in front of a trusted friend, and use breathing techniques before speaking.

Step 7: *How do I feel now?*

This gave her a sense of control and feeling of peace.

By using this practical and powerful tool, Sophia gradually reframed her fear. Instead of seeing public speaking as a trap, she began to see it as an opportunity to grow. She started with small meetings, felt more confident with each success, and eventually delivered a talk at a national conference.

The lesson here is simple: when we question our fearful thoughts, they lose their power. Fear is not the truth - it is only a thought. And thoughts can be changed.

Try It Yourself: Challenging Negative Thoughts

Take a moment to apply this tool to something you currently feel anxious or fearful about. Grab a notebook and gently work through the steps below:

Step 1: *What exactly am I worried/upset/ anxious about?*

Write down the specific situation, or any assumptions about your future, that may be running through your mind and triggering these negative feelings.

Step 2: *What is the worst outcome that can happen in this situation?*

Be honest – what is the scenario you fear most?

Step 3: *How likely is the worst possible scenario going to happen (on a scale of 0–100%)?*

Give it a number. Then pause - does that percentage feel realistic?

Step 4: *What is the evidence that the worst possible outcome will happen?*

When asked this question, many of my clients come

to the realisation that their distress is often driven not by the present moment itself, but by their fearful assumptions rather than facts. Remember: evidence means facts, not your past experiences or your assumptions. Past experiences, while emotionally powerful, are not evidence that the same outcome will occur again; they reflect what happened then, under different circumstances, not what is objectively happening or will happen now.

Now take a few deep breaths, let your body relax, and continue...

Step 5: *What can be the best outcome in this situation? What do I really want to happen?*

Take a moment to visualise the best possible outcome in vivid detail - what it looks like, how it feels, what you are doing, and how others are responding. The more clearly you can picture and describe this ideal scenario, the more powerfully you will activate your focus, motivation, and inner resources to move towards it.

Step 6: *What can I do to attract the best possible outcome?*

Write down practical steps you can take now that will support the positive outcome you want.

Step 7: *How do I feel now?*

Notice how your body and mind feel after going through this process. When all the steps of this cognitive tool are followed with care and honesty, many of my clients report feeling peaceful, joyful, and even enthusiastic when they reach this final question.

The truth is, when your fears begin to dissolve, you naturally open the door to inner peace. When you free yourself from all your fears, you allow your authentic self to shine - the self that is loving, courageous, and deeply connected to life. Then, you will step into the truth of who you really are - not small, limited, or chained, but magnificent, resilient, and free.

How do I Find Peace?

How do I find my peace?
How do I create what I was meant to?
Why suffering when love could be?
Why pain when no guilt should be?

Tell me, oh tell me how have I met the sorrow?
And how have I found the hurt?
Why everybody tells me I ain't chosen and
I ain't worthy?

Why am I longing to find something,
But seeking never reaches anything?
And why am I crying and no tears are falling,
And sadness sets in me day or night?

Peace, my son, is within you,
And you create when you are...
You know the love,
Yet you still let the fear guide you.
And you have sin not,
Yet you let the guilt torment you...

What you are seeking is not outside,
But resides within you...
Has been there ever since your first cry,
Waiting to be found, to be known...

You are worthy as much as you think you are.
So, it is a choice for you to decide upon.
Never ever think you are not chosen,
Because it is a choice for me to decide upon.
And I do choose you.

Dealing Effectively with Negative Emotions

"Anger is a great force. If you can control it, it can be transmitted into a power which can move the whole world."
- Jack Canfield

Q: How can we deal effectively with our negative emotions?

A: Negative emotions, such as anger, fear, hatred, or jealousy, are low-frequency currents of energy that drain our vitality and cloud our minds. If we often experience such negative feelings throughout the day, they will cause inner turbulence, leaving us physically and emotionally exhausted. Consequently, our physical and emotional wellbeing will gradually deteriorate, causing mental health problems or even physical illnesses in the long term. Therefore, it is crucially important to learn how to deal with our emotions effectively and maintain our optimal health and wellbeing.

When people experience any kind of emotion - whether pleasant or unpleasant - they can either suppress it, or express it towards others. Suppressed anger, in particular, is a negative energy that needs to be released, as it causes restlessness, and tension within the body. When you keep suppressing your anger, you are simply postponing the release of the negative energy that is accumulating gradually inside you. Unfortunately, suppressed anger will find its own way to be expressed outward. Therefore, sooner or later, you might end up expressing it towards someone who is weaker or less powerful than you - not because you want to, but because you cannot put up with the enormous amount of negative energy that has been building up within yourself. In doing so, you harm both yourself and others, causing emotional distress for everyone involved. Hence, people who are not able to manage and express their anger in a socially appropriate manner, often struggle to establish and maintain positive and close relationships with others.

Layers of Emotions to Explore

It is important to understand that emotions are rarely one-dimensional. What you feel on the surface, often masks something more vulnerable underneath. Learning to recognise and explore these layers of emotions will help you to respond consciously, rather than react unconsciously.

Let's look more closely at some of the core negative emotions and the deeper truths they reveal.

Anger

Anger often arises when we feel controlled, blocked, disrespected, or treated unfairly. Left unacknowledged, it can turn inward and manifest as self-criticism or depression. Conversely, when expressed outwardly in a socially inappropriate manner, it may take the form of aggression or even violence towards others.

Importantly, anger might mask deeper feelings of fear or sadness. When you feel wounded or rejected, anger can seem like a safer, more powerful response than allowing yourself to show your vulnerability and cry or to admit openly your pain or mistake. Anger may also arise when you feel threatened or powerless, sometimes escalating into rage as a way to reclaim a sense of control in those moments.

When explored with openness and compassion, anger reveals not only your pain but also your need to heal and grow, allowing you to manage it effectively, and to express your needs in a socially appropriate manner.

Sadness

Sadness arises when we sense loss, or feel unable to meet life's demands. If ignored, it may harden into despair, or hopelessness. Yet at its core, sadness reflects our deep yearning for connection, self-care, and self-compassion. At times, it may also conceal feelings of loneliness or guilt. Loneliness often stems from a sense of disconnection with others or the absence of meaningful support. Sadness can also surface when you reflect on your past actions or decisions that you perceive as "wrong" or "inappropriate," bringing you feelings of regret and self-blame.

When embraced with kindness, sadness reveals your longing to reconnect - with yourself, with others, and with life itself.

Fear

Fear is the undercurrent of many emotional struggles: fear of failure, of rejection, of not being good enough. It may drive you to over-control, avoid risks, or strive for perfection in an attempt to feel safe. Yet beneath fear lies the fundamental human need to feel loved, accepted, and secured.

When acknowledged with compassion, fear can become a guide, pointing you towards what most needs healing and reassurance within yourself.

Jealousy

When fear and insecurity mix, jealousy often arises. On the surface, jealousy manifests like resentment towards another person's success, beauty, or relationship. Underneath, however, it often hides a fear of inadequacy, abandonment, or unworthiness. Jealousy can point to your unmet needs for recognition, security, or affirmation.

When explored with honesty, it reveals not only what you envy in others, but also the parts of yourself that long to be healed and the virtues you wish to cultivate.

Hate

At the deepest layer, you may encounter hate - one of the most intense and difficult emotions to face. Hate can emerge as a defense against unbearable hurt, betrayal, or perceived injustice. On the surface, it manifests as rejection or hostility towards others. But beneath it often lies deep pain, humiliation, or a profound sense of vulnerability you've struggled to acknowledge. At times, hate may also mask grief - the sorrow of feeling devalued, powerless, or unseen.

When acknowledged with honesty, hate reveals not only the depth of your pain, but also your deep longing to forgive those who hurt you in the past.

Anxiety

Anxiety is often experienced as restlessness, tension, or a sense of impending danger. But underneath, there may be some deeper emotional layers, such as fear of conflict or rejection, or fear of revealing your vulnerability. For example, you may feel anxious if expressing your anger or asserting your needs feels unsafe or socially unacceptable for you.

Anxiety can also mask feelings of self-doubt, or fear of being exposed. Chronic anxiety may reflect unresolved emotional wounds, repeating themselves in anticipation of danger - even when there's no immediate threat in reality.

When explored with awareness and compassion, anxiety can reveal the areas within you that need healing, and cultivate the courage, resilience, and self-trust to overcome your deepest fears.

Emotion Layer Map: Surface Emotions and Hidden Layers

Surface Emotion	Possible Hidden Layers / Vulnerable Feelings	What It's Really Pointing To / Your Needs	Reader Reflection Prompt
Anger	Hurt, fear, shame, feeling powerless	Longing for fairness, respect, safety, control	*"What am I really feeling beneath this anger?"*
Sadness	Loneliness, guilt, regret, disappointment	Need for connection, self-care, self-compassion	*"What unmet need is my sadness pointing to?"*
Anxiety	Fear of conflict, fear of expressing vulnerability, self-doubt	Need for security, acceptance, reassurance	*"What am I trying to protect myself from?"*
Fear	Insecurity, sense of inadequacy, worry about failure or rejection	Desire for safety, love, acceptance	*"What am I afraid of losing or not having?"*
Jealousy	Insecurity, fear of abandonment, feelings of unworthiness	Need for recognition, affirmation, personal growth	*"What am I longing for that I see in others?"*
Hate	Deep pain, humiliation, grief, unresolved betrayal	Need for healing, justice, protection	*"What hidden pain is this negative feeling trying to communicate?"*

These emotional layers act as protective shields, trying to help you cope with experiences that might otherwise feel too painful or overwhelming. Yet when these hidden emotions remain unacknowledged, they do not disappear. Instead, they continue to influence you quietly from beneath the surface, shaping your thoughts, reactions, and relationships in ways you may not even realise.

By uncovering the hidden roots of your negative emotions, you can begin to transform this destructive energy into healthier forms of expression, such as setting firm boundaries, expressing righteous anger verbally and respectfully, or committing to personal integrity. In doing so, the energy once trapped in pain becomes a force for healing, strength, and growth.

The Shadow and Triggers

Carl Jung, the pioneer of analytical psychology, emphasised that our strongest negative emotions often emerge from what he called the shadow: the hidden part of ourselves where suppressed feelings, insecurities, and unresolved wounds reside. When someone "triggers" us, it isn't only their words or actions that hurt us – it is our shadow reacting. The shadow holds the aspects of ourselves that we are uncomfortable to face: fear of inadequacy, feelings of unworthiness, unresolved grief, jealousy, or shame. When someone "triggers" us, they are like a mirror reflecting something we have buried.

To illustrate this, let's look at a real-life example. Melissa, a 35-year-old marketing manager, felt humiliated when a colleague dismissed her idea during a team meeting. She flushed with anger and felt an overwhelming urge to defend herself, yet something held her back. Instead of reacting, she took a deep breath and quietly asked herself, *"Why does this hurt so much?"*

Through reflection, Melissa realised that her reaction wasn't only about her colleague's comment - it touched a much older wound. As a child, she often felt unseen and unheard in her family, her opinions were usually brushed aside or ignored. That familiar sting of invisibility had resurfaced in that meeting, disguised as anger.

Once Melissa recognised this connection, her perspective began to shift. Rather than criticising herself for being "too sensitive," she saw her anger as a messenger pointing to an unhealed part of herself. By acknowledging this hidden pain with compassion, she started to release its grip. Her emotional trigger became an opportunity for self-understanding, self-compassion and personal growth.

In the days that followed, Melissa began to observe herself more mindfully. Each time she felt dismissed or overlooked, instead of reacting impulsively, she paused, took a breath, and asked herself, *"What part of me feels unseen right now?"* This simple act of awareness helped her separate the present moment from her past wounds.

Melissa also started journaling after emotional triggers, writing down what happened, how she felt, and what deeper memories or beliefs surfaced. Through this practice, she began to notice recurring themes - a deep longing to be valued, heard, and respected. Rather than suppressing these feelings, she allowed herself to feel them fully, often placing her hand on her heart and saying silently, *"It's okay. I see you. I'm listening now."*

Over time, Melissa learned to self-soothe instead of seeking external validation. When faced with criticism, she reminded herself, *"My worth is not defined by others' opinions."* This inner dialogue gradually replaced her old patterns of defensiveness with calm confidence. She even began to practise compassionate communication, expressing her needs clearly but respectfully, for example, saying to a colleague, *"When my ideas are interrupted, I feel unheard. I'd appreciate a chance to finish my thought."* These small but conscious steps helped her rebuild a sense of empowerment and authenticity.

Through this ongoing process of self-awareness, reflection, and gentle self-acceptance, Melissa no longer feared her triggers. They became her mirrors revealing where love and understanding were most needed within herself.

Remember, when you approach your triggers with curiosity instead of judgement, they become your powerful teachers. Recognising this, is the first step towards emotional mastery. Every trigger - whether an impatient driver, a rude coworker, or a critical family member - is a mirror reflecting your shadow, inviting you for deeper self-exploration. As Carl Jung wrote: *"Until you make the unconscious conscious, it will direct your life, and you will call it fate."*

Once you understand that your emotions are not obstacles but your guides in life, you can begin to work with them rather than against them. By listening to what your emotions are trying to tell you, you will open the door to healing, balance, and inner growth.

The following *"Four Steps to Emotional Mastery"* offer a practical path for transforming your emotional pain into clarity, resilience, and personal power.

Four Steps to Emotional Mastery

Step 1: Cultivate Awareness and Acceptance

The first step towards emotional mastery is to become fully aware of your emotions. When a wave of anger, fear, or any unpleasant feeling rises, pause and ask yourself: *"What am I experiencing right now?"* Simply naming the emotion helps you step back and observe it without resistance or escape. With time, you will notice that the intensity of the emotion naturally softens, leaving you with more clarity and calm.

Step 2: Harness the Power of the Pause

When we are triggered, the natural impulse is to react instantly - often without thought. Yet between the trigger and the response there's a small but powerful gap. In that space, you hold the freedom to choose. Many people give this power away, letting others dictate their emotions. But in that pause, you can decide: *"Will I escalate the conflict, step back, or respond calmly and respectfully?"*

Importantly, pausing doesn't mean denying or suppressing what you feel. Instead, it creates room to acknowledge your emotion without letting it take control of your actions. In that moment, you may ask yourself these three grounding questions:

- *What am I thinking right now?*
- *Will I feel better or worse if I do this?*
- *Will this get me closer to what I truly want?*

By reflecting, even briefly, you can shift from an impulsive reaction to a mindful response. This practice of mindfulness - simply observing your thoughts and emotions without immediately acting on them - is a cornerstone of emotional self-mastery.

Step 3: Transform Anger into Love

Anger can be a destructive force - or it can be transformed into a source of compassion and understanding. When anger arises, instead of projecting it on the people or the objects around you, try to focus all your attention on yourself only. You can do this by not paying attention to others in the moments of anger but focusing fully on the centre of your Being - that is located around your heart area.

This simple but powerful technique will immediately bring calmness to your body, as you will connect with the source of peace and love that always resides deep within you. If you remain at this level of awareness long enough, you will begin to feel a gentle warmth around your heart. Gradually, love will spread from your heart into every cell of your body, and soon, your whole Being will be filled with love. This is how you can transform anger into love.

Step 4: Fully Experience All Your Feelings

While anger often grabs our attention, other emotions, like sadness or fear, are equally important. Many people instinctively push these feelings away, distracting themselves with busyness or avoidance. However, avoiding or distracting yourself from grief or fear can prolong your suffering. True healing comes not from escaping from your feelings, but from fully experiencing them.

My client, Caroline, a 29-year-old nurse, often felt overwhelmed by deep sadness after losing some of her patients. She described the feeling as "a heavy ache" in her chest - a quiet pain that lingered long after her shifts ended. In those moments, her instinct was to push the sadness aside, convincing herself that she needed to "stay strong" or "move on." She would scroll through social media for hours, throw herself into extra shifts, or busy herself with small tasks just to avoid sitting with the emptiness inside.

Yet beneath the surface, Caroline often felt exhausted and disconnected. She told me that although she appeared calm and capable, a part of her felt frozen - as if her heart had built a wall to protect itself from more pain. The more she suppressed her grief, the more distant she became from her own emotions and from the people she cared about.

Through counselling, Caroline began to slow down and gently turn towards her inner world. Instead of immediately escaping from her feelings, she practised pausing and asking herself, *What am I feeling right now?"* At first, she found this difficult - tears would rise, and she would feel a wave of sadness and even guilt for "not doing enough" for her patients. But with time, she realised that allowing herself to cry was not a sign of weakness; it was an act of compassion towards herself and her patients.

She began journaling after each emotionally heavy day, writing down her thoughts and memories of the patients she had cared for - their courage, their smiles, their stories. Those quiet moments became her way of honouring their lives, and acknowledging her grief rather than burying it. Gradually, Caroline noticed a lightness returning to her heart. She described feeling more at peace and more present - both with her patients and with her loved ones.

By acknowledging her grief, Caroline discovered that pain - when faced directly - transforms. Her sadness softened into empathy, and her exhaustion gave way to a quiet strength. She no longer needed to run from her emotions; instead, she could meet them with understanding and self-compassion.

Caroline's story shows a profound truth: emotions lose their weight when we stop running from them. By turning towards her sadness instead of avoiding it, Caroline transformed her pain into compassion, and resilience. The same principle applies to all unpleasant emotions - when you accept and process them, they become gateways to inner strength, deeper peace, and authentic connection with yourself and others.

Remember, each emotion you face with awareness becomes your teacher. Each pause you take strengthens your inner resilience. Each act of transformation opens your heart to love. And each time you fully feel, you reclaim your power to live freely and authentically. When you master your emotions, you master your life!

Dealing Effectively
with Stress

"Past and future are in the mind only -
I am now."
- Sri Nisargadatta Maharaj

Q: How can we deal effectively with stress in our modern age?

A: To deal effectively with stress in life, first we need to deepen our self-understanding. In particular, we need to understand the workings of our own mind. As Sogyal Rinpoche wisely observed, *"It is vital to familiarise yourself with the nature of mind while you are still alive."* This wisdom reminds us that much of our stress does not come from external events themselves, but from how our minds perceive them, and react to them.

It is important to understand that the human mind has a natural inclination to focus predominantly on the negative. For instance, if you receive ten compliments and one negative remark in a single day - which one will you remember most vividly? Most of us would remember the negative one.

Another tendency of the mind is to dwell on the past, or to rush ahead into the future. There is nothing wrong with looking back on your life, and it is also important to plan your future. However, when you remain stuck in either, you sacrifice the peace and joy available to you in the present moment. The more time you spend thinking about the past or the future, the more mental energy you will consume, and eventually, more stressed and tired you will feel by the end of the day.

The reasoning here is that when you are thinking about the past, usually you regret it, and that can leave you feeling sad, disappointed, or even angry. On other occasions, you may glorify your past. Even if you are glorifying it, you might still experience sadness inside, believing that your past was better than your life now. On the other hand, when your mind is in the future, you're more likely to feel anxious, fearful, or worried whether life will unfold according to your expectations. Hence, thoughts about the past or the future are the robbers of your precious time in the present moment.

In my work with clients from all around the world, I've observed that stress often stems from the mind's constant preoccupation with the past or worries about the future. A clear example of this is my client Lily, in her fifties, who often found herself replaying memories of her failed marriage. Every morning, her thoughts would drift to what she "should have said" or "could have done differently." Feelings of guilt, sadness and self-blame would rise, whispering that she wasn't good enough. At times, she caught herself longing for the moments when her life felt easier, believing that her best days were already behind her. These thoughts left her emotionally exhausted and disconnected from the simple joys of her present life.

Through counselling, Lily learned to use a powerful technique called the *"Focused Breathing Exercise"* (explained at the end of this chapter), which she used whenever her thoughts drifted to the past. Each time she practised mindful breathing, she noticed how her body relaxed, and her mind grew quieter. After each session of mindful breathing, Lily would gently repeat few empowering affirmations such as:

- *"I can learn from my past, but I am not defined by it."*

- *"In this moment, I choose peace."*
- *"I am fully present now."*
- *"I will approach this activity with joy."*

With consistent practice, Lily began to feel lighter. She discovered that anchoring herself in the present, allowed her to carry the wisdom of the past without being imprisoned by it. As she released her regrets from the past, she felt a growing sense of hope, and emotional freedom.

Mike, a young professional, faced the opposite challenge. His mind was constantly racing ahead, filled with endless "what if" scenarios about his career and future. *"What if I fail?" "What if I make the wrong decision?" "What if I'm not good enough?"* These questions looped endlessly in his mind, tightening his chest and keeping him awake at night. Even on his days off, he found it difficult to relax. His thoughts were always one step ahead - planning, predicting, or fearing what might come next. Over time, this mental overactivity drained his energy, and robbed him of the joy in everyday moments.

In counselling, Mike learned to calm this inner turbulence through the *"Focused Breathing Exercise."* Each morning and evening, he practised slowing his breath and bringing his awareness back to the present moment. After calming his mind, he would affirm empowering statements such as:

- *"I am capable of handling whatever comes my way."*
- *"I trust myself to make the best decisions, one step at a time."*
- *"I release all my worries, and embrace the present moment fully."*

Gradually, Mike noticed a shift. His thoughts no longer controlled him; he could observe them without getting swept away. His sleep deepened, his focus sharpened, and he began to approach both work and life with greater calm, confidence, and trust.

To live more peacefully, you need to bless your past, make peace with it, and release it - if it keeps you in bondage. You also need to bless your future - trusting that it will bring you great opportunities, growth, and joy. The secret lies in remembering that the present moment is all you truly have. It is the only time when you are truly alive, and capable of creating change. When you ground yourself in the present, you allow peace to fill your heart, and clarity to guide your path forward.

One of the simplest, yet most profound ways to return to the present moment is by focusing on your breath. Breath is life. Breath is the bridge between your body and your mind. When you focus your full attention on the breath itself, it will naturally bring your mind into the present moment. By learning to pay undivided attention to your breath, you will relax deeply, alleviate your stress immediately, and quiet your mind naturally.

The following scientifically proven technique called *"Focused Breathing Exercise"* is a very simple, yet powerful tool that can help you return to the present moment and connect deeply with yourself.

Focused Breathing Exercise

1. Take a comfortable position, and either close your eyes or rest them gently on a fixed spot in the room.

2. Take a few slow, deep breaths. Allow all your muscles to relax and release any tension in your body.

3. Notice the sounds around you. Gently set aside any thoughts, judgements, or opinions. Just be...

4. Now, bring all your attention to your breath. Breathe slowly...deeply...effortlessly... Be aware of your breathing. Notice the cool air entering your nostrils... and the warm air leaving your body... Feel the rhythm of life moving through you - the rise and fall of your chest, the gentle expansion and contraction of your abdomen...

All you need to do is watch it happening. There is no need to control anything. Just allow the breath to flow naturally - softly, peacefully, as it always has. You are simply the witness... observing the dance of inhalation and exhalation, the body breathing by itself, each breath arriving and leaving in its own time. There is no strain, no effort involved - only awareness.

5. Now, begin to notice the brief pause - that still, silent space between two breaths.

As you exhale, allow the breath to empty naturally... not forcing, not controlling... simply letting it fall away. At the very end of each exhalation, notice the moment where nothing moves - a tiny oasis of stillness, a perfect rest before the next inhalation gently rises on its own.

Then follow the inhalation as it fills you softly and steadily... and at its peak - sense the second pause - a light, suspended moment where the breath is full, the body quiet, and awareness completely present. Let your attention rest in these sacred intervals. The pause after the exhalation... the pause after the inhalation... each one a doorway to the silence within you. Allow yourself to sink into these spaces as if they were warm, welcoming rooms... Feel how the mind grows quieter there, how the body softens, how the heart gently opens. With every cycle of breathing, you are invited back into these timeless gaps - the still points that exist between effort and ease, between doing and being.

Notice the calm that begins to spread from these pauses... a sense of spaciousness, a subtle depth of peace, as though something ancient and steady is awakening within you. In these pauses, nothing is demanded of you. Nothing is missing. Nothing needs to be fixed. There is only the quiet presence of your own Being - vast, peaceful, and always here. Rest in this silence between each breath and allow the stillness to reveal itself breath after breath moment after moment.

6. Remain focused on these gaps for a few breathing cycles...

7. When you are ready, you may open your eyes, feeling energised, relaxed, and calm. Carry the sense of calm and spaciousness with you throughout the day.

If you'd like to practise quieting your mind and returning to the present moment, you can find a guided focused breathing exercise with my gentle voice on my YouTube channel, *Dr Snezhana,* titled *"5 -Minute Slow Breathing Exercise to Calm Your Mind with Dr Snezhana."* This simple, soothing exercise can help you release tension, restore inner balance, and reconnect with the calm power of the present moment. With regular practice, this breathing technique can help you meet life's challenges with clarity, patience, and resilience.

Remember, in every moment you have a choice - to be pulled by the past, driven by the future, or anchored in the now. When you choose the present, you reclaim your own power. Moreover, with each mindful breath, you declare that your peace no longer depends on external circumstances - it flows from within. You return home to your own calm, your own strength. You emerge lighter, clearer, and more empowered.

So, take a deep breath, lift your heart, and step forward with trust. You are no longer surviving your days - you are living them - fully, consciously, and freely.

The Mind and the Heart

There is a game, some call it life
In which you decide who guides you,
Which one is to be followed,
And which one is to be led.

You may choose your mind
To guide you through the game,
And very soon you find yourself
In a swirly maze with no exit doors.

In such a game which you call "my life"
There's only sorrow and despair,
Only grief for the past, and fear for the future.
No place for peace and wisdom, no song, nor dance.

You think that if your mind decides
You can't go astray,
Because your mind remembers and recounts,
Calculates and resets.

But your mind knows nothing of your real you,
Because you are not your mind.
Your mind knows nothing of who you really are,
Because this knowing cannot be learnt.

Yet you may choose your heart
To guide you through this game,
And very soon you find yourself
In an open space with countless doors.

In this game, which then is called life
There is only joy and gladness.
There is no past or future,
Only now and here exists.

You feel that if your heart decides
You experience it all,
Because your heart rejoices and sings,
Just because of its own joy and song.

Your heart knows everything about you,
Because you are love which only lives in your heart.
And only through love you truly experience yourself,
And this experience can only be beheld...

Experiencing True Freedom

"I want freedom for the full expression
of my personality."
- Mahatma Gandhi

Q: How can we achieve true freedom in our lives?

A: Every human being carries within an infinite Being with an infinite energy and a limitless power, but that Being feels imprisoned. This prison is not imposed by the world but built through people's self-limiting beliefs and self-imposed fears. So, no matter where they go, most people carry this invisible prison with them. As a result, they suffer, because they are afraid of the false image they have created about themselves. This self-constructed image confines them, shaping their actions and behaviours to meet others' expectations rather than reflecting their true essence. Consequently, many people are afraid to connect deeply with their true self or with another human being. So, they struggle to express their true potential, to experience genuine romantic love, or to build meaningful friendships.

It is important to understand that most of these self-limiting beliefs are formed during the first seven years of life, through the interactions with our parents, teachers, and other influential figures. As children, we trust these significant people completely, without questioning the ideas, rules, and judgements they instil in us. Therefore, we grow up absorbing their words as unquestionable truths.

Sadly, many people continue to live without ever examining these inherited beliefs. Yet these beliefs act as a lens through which you perceive yourself, others, and the world. Often, they appear as inner voices that criticise, doubt, or diminish you - voices that quietly shape your choices, relationships, and your sense of worth. Over time, they can limit your potential and interfere with your happiness and success in life.

For this reason, it is vital to realise that when you live according to others' beliefs, you live in conflict with your genuine self. And when you constantly fight against your true nature, your energy becomes scattered - you end each day feeling drained, not because life is too demanding, but because you are living against your own truth.

To illustrate how these early beliefs can shape our adult life, let's look at Valentino's story. Valentino, 42, grew up in a highly critical household where praise was rare and mistakes were magnified. His parents believed that constant correction would make him stronger and more successful. But to a sensitive child, their criticism didn't build resilience - it built shame. Each time his achievements went unnoticed or his efforts were met with disapproval, a painful message began to take root in his young mind: *"I cannot be loved and accepted as I am. So, I must prove my worth."*

This belief quietly guided much of Valentino's life. As an adult, he worked tirelessly to earn others' approval - striving for perfection at work, pleasing his romantic partners, and avoiding mistakes at all costs. On the surface, he appeared responsible, and calm, but inside he carried a deep fear of failure and rejection. Every small error felt like proof that he wasn't good enough.

In his romantic relationships, he found it difficult to relax and trust love. Even when his romantic partners reassured him, he questioned their sincerity, thinking, *"If they really knew me, they wouldn't stay."* Professionally, he often downplayed his abilities, hesitating to apply for promotions or share his ideas, convinced that his colleagues were more capable. His happiness always felt conditional - tied to his achievement, external validation, or others' approval. Over time, this quiet inner struggle drained Valentino's joy and self-confidence. For him, life felt like an endless race to earn the unconditional love and respect he longed for from those around him.

In our counselling sessions, he began to recognise that this harsh inner voice was not truly his own - it was an echo from his childhood. By bringing these subconscious beliefs into his awareness, he started to see them for what they were: shadows from the past, not reflections of his truth. We worked together to challenge and replace these old patterns through daily affirmations - not as hollow words, but as conscious acts of self-compassion.

Valentino learned to speak to himself gently, with presence, as if comforting a dear friend. His new, empowering statements included:

- *"I am learning to see myself through kind and loving eyes."*
- *"My worth is not earned - it already exists within me."*
- *"Each day, I grow stronger, wiser, and more confident in who I am."*

At first, these words felt unfamiliar, even uncomfortable - his old beliefs resisted them. But through determination, daily repetition, and mindful reflection, something within him began to soften. He noticed that when the inner critic spoke, he could pause, take a breath, and choose a kinder response. Gradually, that critical voice lost its power. Valentino described the change beautifully: *"It's like I've stopped being at war with myself. I finally feel like I'm on my own side."*

As he began to treat himself with more compassion, understanding, and respect, new possibilities opened up for him. He applied for a leadership role at work, rekindled some old friendships, and started exploring creative interests he had long abandoned. Most importantly, he discovered that genuine happiness didn't come from proving his worth - it came from accepting it.

Remember that most of your limiting beliefs are concepts learnt from others that can exist only in darkness. Once they are brought to light, they lose their power because they are not real - they are just borrowed shadows. Once you release these unhelpful beliefs, you will begin to see the world with your own eyes, and perceive yourself with fresh clarity. Then, you will uncover the truth about your existence and, with it, your infinite possibilities. As Dr Wayne Dyer beautifully wrote, *"The only limits you have - are the limits you believe."*

Below are some common limiting beliefs that can interfere with your happiness and success in life, along with practical ways to transform them:

- **Limiting belief:** *"I should be approved and loved by every significant person in my life."*

- **New empowering belief:** *"I release the need for approval from others. Their judgements and opinions reflect their own perceptions. My worth is not measured by anyone's opinion. What truly matters is that I love, accept, and respect myself."*

- **Limiting belief:** *"The past, and all its mistakes, defines me and ruins my present moment."*

- **New empowering belief:** *"Mistakes are lessons, not chains. I cannot change the past, but I can shape my future. I can learn from yesterday, and live fully today. Each new moment offers me a great opportunity to begin again."*

- **Limiting belief:** *"I must be competent and successful at everything I attempt."*

- **New empowering belief:** *"Competence comes with practice. I give myself permission to experiment, learn, and grow - even if I'm not perfect at first. Every step forward matters. Joy is found in the process, not just in the outcome."*

Now, turn your attention inward and take a moment to reflect on your own life. What beliefs about yourself have you accepted in the past without question? Are there any inner voices that still echo the criticism or doubt of others - perhaps whispering that you are not good enough, not capable enough, or not deserving of love, happiness and success? Remember, these beliefs may have guided your choices for years, yet they are not your truth. As you bring them into awareness, you gain the freedom to choose differently - to replace self-judgement with self-understanding, fear with trust, and self-doubt with self-compassion.

Each time you challenge a limiting belief - you reclaim a piece of your authentic power and move closer to living as the person you were always meant to be. You realise that you are not your thoughts, nor your past, nor the expectations placed upon you. You are the awareness beneath them all - steady, peaceful, and infinitely capable of renewal. When you live from your authentic self, you no longer seek freedom - you become it.

I am Free

I drop all my beliefs.
I do not have any expectations.
I do not regret anything.
I feel good about myself.
I accept everything without any judgement.
I accept whatever comes
Because I know that
The Universe knows what's best for me.
I am grateful for everything.
I am free...

Improving Self-Esteem and Finding Self-Worth

"What lies behind us and what lies before us are tiny matters compared to what lies within us."
- Ralph Waldo Emerson

Q: How can I improve my low self-esteem and find self-worth?

A: Most of us carry a story we have created about ourselves - a story that shapes our self-image. This self-image, formed during our early childhood through the interactions with our parents or caregivers, becomes the lens through which we see ourselves. The truth is that our self-image deeply influences our self-esteem - how we feel about our own worth.

When your self-image is distorted or rooted in early wounds, you may find yourself overly concerned with how others see you - wondering whether you are liked, accepted, or "good enough." Sadly, such patterns obscure your true essence and prevent you from seeing your inner beauty. Hence, you may struggle to love and accept yourself as you truly are.

Instead, guided by this false self-image, you will act in ways that will not reflect your authentic self, thus creating an inner conflict between who you think you should be and who you really are. Therefore, it is important to become aware of the traits and patterns that belong to this false sense of self on which you ordinarily act in life. In doing so, you will open space for genuine self-acceptance, unconditional self-love, and the freedom to express your true self in the world.

The following section explores four common personality patterns that create a false sense of self and low self-esteem, along with practical strategies and real-life stories that illustrate how they can be transformed.

The Perfectionist - *"I have to do everything perfectly"*

Perfectionists tend to have high expectations, are self-critical, and are hard on themselves. They exhibit a strong need for control and precision, and experience distress when their achievements fall short of their rigid expectations. This can create problems in their lives, as they can be easily disappointed with themselves and the people around them, when their high expectations have not been met. Perfectionists often become preoccupied with their actions and behaviours, which can leave them feeling tense, anxious, and overly serious about life. By putting so much pressure on themselves to do everything perfectly, they are not on the right path to self-fulfilment and self-realisation, but on the path to burnout.

Perfectionism demands that they and their work are flawless and absolutely perfect, as anything else is unacceptable for them. It is either black or white - either they are perfect, or they are a failure. Holding on the belief to be perfect is self-destructive and soul-destroying. By being perfectionists, they are constantly blaming themselves for their failures, while trying to reach perfection.

The need to be perfect is based on fear that if they do not succeed in all their endeavours, they are not good enough. The main reason for being a perfectionist is a low self-concept, and a low self-esteem. Perfectionists cannot accept that they are good enough as they really are - with all their imperfections and flaws. Thus, they always find mistakes, no matter how well they are doing, or how good they have done their work.

The perfectionist's main focus is on the achievement and the outcome, and not on the process itself. Therefore, they are not really enjoying what they are doing. Because perfectionists have very ambitious goals and high expectations, which often are unrealistic, they will never feel that they have achieved enough. This in turn, makes their feelings of inadequacy and incompetence even worse.

Many perfectionists struggle silently, appearing successful while feeling drained inside. Grace's experience shows how this pattern can unfold in real life. Grace, a 42-year-old architect, came to counselling feeling utterly exhausted. On paper, she was successful - a respected professional with multiple design awards and a steady stream of high-profile clients. Yet inside, she felt empty. *"No matter how much I achieve,"* she admitted, *"it never feels like I am good enough."*

Her perfectionism had quietly taken control of every part of her life. She spent long nights obsessing over every detail of her designs, constantly revising her drawings until the early morning hours. Even when her clients were thrilled, Grace would fixate on minor flaws that no one else noticed. *"If my designs aren't perfect,"* she said, *"I feel like a fraud."*

In therapy, Grace discovered that her drive for perfection stemmed from a deep -seated belief that her worth depended entirely on her achievements. As a child, she often received praise only when she excelled - not for who she was, but for what she did. She carried this pattern into adulthood, feeling that resting meant that she was failing and that any imperfection was something to be ashamed of.

Together, we began to gently challenge these unhelpful beliefs. Grace learned to pause when she caught herself spiralling into self-criticism and ask, *"Who am I trying to please right now - my clients or my inner critic?"* She practised submitting projects that were "good enough" instead of endlessly revising them. At first, this felt uncomfortable, even risky, but soon, she noticed that her clients were still satisfied, and she had more time and energy for herself.

To support this shift, Grace kept a *"Self-kindness Log,"* noting each moment she allowed imperfection without judgement - whether it was leaving a sketch unfinished or declining extra work to rest. She also began repeating affirmations, such as:

- *Every small and imperfect step I take, moves me closer to my goals.*

- *I choose progress and purpose over perfection.*

- *I focus on the process, not just the outcome, finding joy and meaning in every step of the journey.*

- *By being fully engaged and joyful in each moment, I experience a sense of flow and fulfillment that transcends results.*

- *My mistakes are not failures - each challenge teaches me how to rise stronger and smarter.*

At the beginning, she noticed that even simple sketches that were not "perfect" felt strange to value. Yet with practice, she began to see the beauty in the process itself - enjoying the movement of her pencil, the flow of new ideas, and the act of creating without immediately judging the result. She started to appreciate her drawings as expressions of her creativity, not as tests of her worth. Each imperfect sketch became a small victory, a reminder that creation could be joyful even without perfection.

Gradually, the pressure began to lift. Grace started enjoying her creative process again - sketching freely, exploring bold new ideas, and even laughing at her earlier obsession with "flawless" designs. She told me one day, *"I used to design to prove my worth. Now I design because I love creating."*

Grace's story reminds us that perfectionism may steal your joy by tying your self-worth to performance. Freedom begins when you shift the focus from flawless outcomes to the beauty of the process itself - and learn that being "enough" is not something to earn, but something to remember.

If you feel that you might be a perfectionist, you need to examine your inner core beliefs about yourself. Ask yourself:

- *Do you often feel the need to prove yourself to those around you?*

- *Do you think that if you don't push yourself so hard, others won't love or appreciate you?*

If you answered affirmatively to these questions, it's time to gently challenge the unhelpful assumptions that fuel your perfectionism. Start by questioning the truth behind these beliefs. Ask yourself:

- *Who taught me that I must be perfect to be worthy of love or respect?*
- *What evidence do I have that other people only value me for my achievements?*
- *How might my life feel if I allowed myself to be human - imperfect, yet whole?*

Each time you notice perfectionistic thoughts such as *"I must not make mistakes"* or *"I have to be better than others,"* pause and replace them with a more compassionate truth: *"It's okay to make mistakes - that's how I learn and grow. My worth is not defined by comparison with others."*

The most powerful way to break free from perfectionism is to release the limiting belief that you must be flawless and to embrace the truth that you are already perfect in your imperfection - whole, lovable, and loving just as you are. Your worth is not defined by perfect outcomes, but by your courage, authenticity, and willingness to grow. When you begin to value progress over perfection and authenticity over approval, you create space for true peace, creativity, and joy to flourish.

The Naysayer - *"I can't"*

The naysayer is a person who generally expresses negative or pessimistic views and often engages in excessive complaining or a consistently downbeat attitude. Naysayers are quick to deny possibilities, criticise ideas, and to cast doubts on themselves and others. They tend to be sceptical, cynical, and frequently discourage those around them from pursuing their goals or dreams.

In essence, a naysayer can act as a dream killer or a faith killer. Their habitual phrases - such as, *"That's a bad idea,"* or *"This will never work"* - reflect an underlying mindset that assumes failure and hopelessness. This way of thinking generates negative energy, spreading frustration, anxiety, and even anger to those in their environment. To a naysayer, opportunities seem limited, challenges appear insurmountable, and optimism is often dismissed. They unconsciously prefer the safety of certainty, even if it is bleak, rather than the risk of the unknown.

If you recognise these tendencies in yourself, it can be helpful to see how someone else faced similar challenges and gradually overcame them. William, a 29-year-old IT professional, often began our counselling sessions with phrases like, *"That won't work,"* or *"I'll never manage that."* On the surface, he appeared confident, but underneath, he felt stuck and frustrated. He described himself as someone who *"kills his own dreams before they even start."*

When we explored this further, William realised that his constant negativity wasn't laziness or lack of ambition - it was self-protection. By expecting failure, he avoided the deeper fear of trying and not being good enough. He believed that if he never aimed high, he could never be disappointed. This mindset had become a form of emotional armour that kept him "safe" but also trapped in stagnation.

In our sessions, William began noticing the language he used with himself. Phrases like *"I can't,"* *"It's too hard,"* or *"Others are just better than me"* reflected a pattern of self-sabotage. Together, we worked on identifying these automatic thoughts and replacing them with more balanced, empowering ones. Instead of jumping to conclusions about failure, he began asking himself, *"What if this works out?"* or *"What's one small step I can take today that will bring me closer to my goal?"*

To reinforce this shift, William kept a small notebook where he recorded some positive affirmations, as well as evidence of his progress, such as:

- *"Every step I take - no matter how small - shapes my future success."*
- *"I am capable of learning, growing and becoming stronger with every experience."*
- *"I choose to focus on what's possible rather than what's missing."*
- *"Opportunities are everywhere I look."*
- *"I uplift those around me with words of encouragement, support, and genuine hope."*

He also began practising short breathing exercises whenever he caught himself spiralling into negativity. This helped him pause, reset, and respond more calmly to his self-critical thoughts.

Gradually, these small changes, built confidence in him. Within a few months, William felt ready to take on something he had long dismissed as "impossible" - applying for a leadership program at his company. The "old William" would have talked himself out of it, convinced he wasn't "leadership material." But this time, he reminded himself, *"I just need to try. If I try, I won't lose anything. But I have the chance to gain something valuable for my future - new skills, self-confidence, and a proof that I am capable of more than I imagined."* To his surprise, not only did he apply - but he was also accepted. The moment he received the acceptance email, he said, *"For the first time in my life, I feel like I'm not standing on my own way."*

William's journey shows that real change begins when you challenge your inner critic, take small steps despite fear, and start believing that change is possible.

If you recognise these traits in yourself, you need to understand that your own fears create your reality and may affect others in a negative way. Hence, it is important to identify and become increasingly aware of your own fears that unconsciously, you are projecting on others as well. You might be scared that others may achieve their goals and succeed in life, while you have not been able to achieve yours. However, if you continue to act out of your fears, you won't be able to accomplish your goals and realise your full potential in life. Don't deny yourself of the life you deserve to live because of your fears!

What you need to do is to tune in, look deep within yourself, and think about the ideal vision of your life. Reflect on what you truly want to achieve and what feels most meaningful to you. Then, focus your attention on those goals that genuinely matter to you, and do your best to pursue them. When you pursue goals that align with your inner values, your life naturally gains a deeper sense of purpose, and you begin to feel more fulfilled and confident in yourself. At the same time, when others share their dreams and goals with you, choose to be encouraging, supportive, and helpful. Your kindness and belief in them can inspire their growth and success, just as you pursue your own.

When you shift from doubt to possibility, from fear to faith, life begins to open in remarkable ways. You start to see that every dream carries the seed of growth, and every challenge hides an opportunity to expand beyond your limitations. As you cultivate trust in yourself and in life's unfolding, your inner dialogue transforms from *"I can't"* to *"I'm willing to try."*

Remember, courage is not the absence of fear - it is the decision to move forward despite it. Each time you take a step towards your vision, no matter how small, you weaken the grip of self-doubt and strengthen the voice of hope within you. Over time, that hopeful voice becomes your guiding light - leading you towards a life filled with purpose, confidence, and joy.

And as you walk this path, your energy becomes contagious. By believing in your own potential, you naturally inspire others to believe in theirs. Together, you create a ripple of encouragement that uplifts not only your world but the world around you.

The Doubter - *"What if I fail?"*

A doubter is a person who constantly questions the truth or existence of something and requires solid, physical proof before believing it. Doubters tend to be highly sceptical and often lack faith in themselves. They view every important decision as a kind of test - one in which they fear they might fall short. As a result, they frequently seek advice from others, find it difficult to trust their own judgement, and may change their minds repeatedly. Even after making a decision, they often continue to worry, questioning whether they made the right choice.

At the heart of self-doubt lies a negative self-concept and low self-esteem. Chronic anxiety often accompanies this mindset, creating a sense of uncertainty and a feeling of having little control over one's life. The resulting hesitation can prevent personal growth and achievement, as self-doubt becomes a barrier to taking meaningful actions in life.

Leah, a 36-year-old high school teacher, knew this all too well. She constantly worried about whether she was "good enough" for her students. Even after receiving praise from their parents, her colleagues, and the principal of the school, her focus remained on her perceived shortcomings. *"What if I fail them?"* she asked repeatedly, unable to silence the anxious voice in her head. At work, this self-doubt made her overly cautious. She was hesitant to try new teaching methods, and to share her ideas with her peers, fearing that she might get it "wrong."

Leah began to challenge these ingrained beliefs by practising positive self-talk. Each time self-doubt crept in, she reminded herself: *"I am doing my best, and that is more than enough. I may not know everything yet, but I'm learning and improving every day. I trust my intuition and my ability to make wise decisions."* She also kept a journal to record moments of competence and small successes, from effectively managing a challenging class to receiving simple words of thanks from a student. Over time, these practices strengthened her self-trust.

Gradually, Leah regained confidence in her abilities. She started taking initiative in her classroom, experimenting with new teaching approaches, and sharing her ideas with colleagues. The transformation went beyond her professional life - she became more assertive, self-assured, and willing to take risks. Eventually, Leah not only reclaimed her self-confidence but also began mentoring new teachers, helping them navigate their own challenges with self-doubt.

Leah's journey illustrates a key lesson: self-doubt can feel paralysing, but by practising positive self-talk, and celebrating even small victories, anyone can cultivate self-belief, resilience, and a sense of empowerment.

If you identify with this pattern, the first step is to recognise your negative beliefs and the negative self-talk that reinforces them. Self-doubt cannot be overcome without cultivating faith in yourself - and the foundation of that faith lies in the words you choose to speak to yourself. Remember, words are powerful - they can either magnify self-doubt or nurture self-confidence. Believing you will fail often guarantees failure; conversely, expecting positive outcomes opens the door to new possibilities and growth.

Faith is not just an abstract idea; it is a living quality that can be cultivated. One of the most potent ways to strengthen it is through feminine receptivity - a gentle, open awareness of the Universe and the subtle signs it offers when you are faced with important decisions. By listening deeply, observing quietly, and trusting the guidance that presents itself, you allow your inner wisdom to align with the flow of life. This receptive, intuitive approach does not demand force or control; instead, it nurtures trust in yourself, in timing, and in the unseen support around you.

As you practise this openness, your words and your expectations begin to shift naturally. You start to notice the synchronicities, the small affirmations, and the moments of clarity that guide your choices. With each step, faith grows - not as a rigid certainty, but as a quiet, steady trust in your ability to navigate life, to make wise decisions, and to create the outcomes you truly desire.

It is also crucial to acknowledge and celebrate your progress. Doubters tend to focus on their perceived shortcomings or they set excessively high expectations for themselves, which leads them to overlook their achievements. Know that minimising or ignoring progress can cause hesitation and withdrawal from further efforts. By intentionally recognising even small successes, you reinforce self-belief and cultivate momentum. Remember that every effort, no matter how small, is an essential step forward!

Finally, it is important to confront the underlying fears that may arise when positive change begins to manifest. These fears are natural but can be transformed through conscious awareness and the practice of self-affirmation. Self-doubt doesn't disappear overnight - it softens each time you choose self-trust over fear. Every time you speak kindly to yourself, act despite uncertainty, or celebrate a small success, you are rewriting the story of your life - from *"What if I fail?"* to *"What if I soar?"* By learning to support yourself through life's challenges, and learn from your mistakes, you can gradually shift from a mindset of self-doubt to one of self-empowerment, self-trust, and personal fulfillment.

The Procrastinator - *"I'll do it tomorrow"*

A procrastinator is a person who is delaying, putting off, or avoiding doing the task that needs to be accomplished in a timely manner. Procrastinators have a habit of engaging in more pleasurable activities instead of doing less pleasurable tasks. They are also more likely to carry out less urgent tasks instead of more urgent ones, thus putting off impending tasks to a later time. Over time, this pattern can negatively affect their professional success, as well as their relationships with others.

Procrastination is linked to low self-esteem, anxiety, depression, and poor study habits. It may result in causing stress, a sense of guilt, loss of productivity, and a social disapproval for not meeting one's responsibilities.

Notably, perfectionism and procrastination are very closely related as perfectionism often underlies the fear of failure. If parents' expectations are too high that no one could actually live up to them, procrastination might take place to derail parental expectations and standards. Procrastination may be a way to cope with the family pressure to constantly be good enough. If people find themselves rebelling against their parents, it often means they have allowed their parents to hold a great deal of power in their lives - probably more than they really want. In such cases, procrastination becomes a symbolic attempt to regain control over one's own life.

Fear of success can be another possible reason for procrastination. For example, if one's success opens a door to higher expectations, one can procrastinate because they are fearful that if they do well, then next time, even more would be expected of them.

To illustrate how procrastination can take hold and be overcome, let's consider the story of Tim. Tim, a 27-year-old university student, came to therapy feeling overwhelmed and stuck under the weight of his unfinished assignments. He described a familiar cycle: instead of starting his work, he would scroll through social media, play video games, or distract himself with minor tasks. *"If I don't start, I can't fail,"* he admitted. But in reality, this avoidance left him feeling anxious, guilty, and constantly behind. His self-criticism grew louder with every passing deadline, reinforcing a sense of helplessness and frustration within himself.

In our sessions, we explored the reasons behind his procrastination. Tim realised that fear of imperfection played a major role - he worried that his essays wouldn't be good enough and that his poor performance would disappoint both himself and others. He also noticed how much pressure he had internalised from family expectations and academic standards, which made starting any task feel daunting.

To break the cycle, Tim experimented with reframing his inner dialogue. Instead of saying, *"I should do this,"* he began telling himself, *"I choose to start this task with one small, imperfect step. Every step I take, no matter how small, moves me closer to my goals and dreams."* This shift from obligation to choice helped him feel more in control and less paralysed by anxiety. He also implemented a system of rewards: after completing a focused 45-minute work session, he allowed himself a short break, a small treat, or a few minutes to relax.

Tim also learned to break large assignments into manageable chunks. Instead of attempting to tackle an entire paper in one sitting, he set mini-goals: outlining, drafting a single section, or editing one paragraph at a time. Each completed step gave him tangible proof of progress, which gradually replaced his self-doubt with self-confidence.

Over several weeks, Tim's new approach transformed his academic habits. He finished his assignments on time, felt less anxious about his deadlines, and began to experience a sense of pride and competence. More importantly, he discovered that taking small, imperfect action - starting even when he feared failure - was far more productive than waiting for the "perfect moment."

Tim's story illustrates a key principle: procrastination often masks fear and perfectionism, but by taking small, intentional steps, reframing one's self-talk, and celebrating progress, anyone can regain control, build confidence, and achieve meaningful goals in life.

If you recognise procrastination in yourself, the first step is to reclaim your personal power and intentionally decide what you want for your life, rather than reacting to the demands or expectations of others. Understanding that perfectionism fuels procrastination is essential: you must allow yourself to be imperfect and embrace the possibility of taking small, flawed steps. Remember, you can always revise, improve, and refine your work later.

Language and mindset are key tools for overcoming procrastination. Phrases like *"I should do this"* often create internal resistance. Instead, reframe your thinking with *"I choose to..."* For example, you may say: *"I choose to start this task with one small step. While doing it, I'll enjoy the process, while feeling good within, and leaving room for relaxation and fun afterwards."*

Incorporating small rewards, breaks, and moments of gratitude throughout your tasks, reinforces positive behaviour, reduces resistance, and makes progress more enjoyable. By shifting your focus from obligation to choice, and from perfection to process, you regain control over your time, and cultivate a sense of accomplishment and self-worth.

Each of these self-imposed masks - the Perfectionist, the Naysayer, the Doubter, and the Procrastinator - was born from the inner story that whispers, *"I am not enough as I am."* Yet the truth is profoundly different: your worth is not measured by your flawless performance, by your fears, or by your self-doubt. It has always existed within you.

When you begin to gently question the beliefs that sustain these patterns, and practise new, empowering ways of thinking, you start to dissolve the layers that have long obscured your true essence. In that unfolding, something profound begins to happen - your self-esteem and self-worth no longer depend on achievements, approval, or comparison. They arise naturally, from within, as you remember your inherent wholeness. You no longer need to prove your value to the world - you simply embody it. By embracing, knowing, and honouring the truth of who you really are, you return home to yourself - peaceful, radiant, and free.

Dissolving the Ego

"You only are if you stop thinking."
- Osho

Q: Understanding that the ego is the source of all conflicts and problems in life, the question is how can we dissolve the ego?

A: Ego is a false sense of self - a construct formed through our unconscious identification with the mind. It is made up of all the beliefs we hold about ourselves and the world, most of which were acquired from others long before we had the capacity to question them. Accepted early in life and reinforced through constant repetition, these borrowed beliefs eventually harden into what we perceive as unquestionable truth. We believe because we were taught to believe.

Yet it is essential to recognise that every ego-based belief is rooted in fear. From this fear arise our negative thoughts, our painful emotions, and ultimately the suffering that keeps us from knowing our true, inner self.

Here are some of the most common ego beliefs people hold about themselves:

- *I am what I do. My job and professional achievements define me.*

- *I am what I have. My material possessions define me.*

- *I am what others think of me. My self-image - imposed by others - defines me.*

- *I am separate from everything and everyone in the world. My physical body defines me alone.*

Your ignorance lies in believing that you are the ego. However, the ego is never at rest - it lives in perpetual desire, always seeking, always wanting, always grasping for more. It hungers for external forms of power: money, recognition, material comforts, or social status. There is nothing inherently wrong in earning money or striving for professional success. But when your identity becomes tied to these external things or achievements - or to a self-image shaped by the expectations of others - you inevitably lose touch with your true self.

Many people live this way without realising it - unconsciously equating their worth with what they achieve or possess. One such person was Edmond, a 42-year-old lawyer who believed that his entire value came from his professional status. For most of his adult life, his identity revolved around being "a successful attorney." Edmond's sense of worth depended on how others perceived him - on winning cases, being admired, and maintaining a flawless image of competence. Deep down, he carried an unexamined belief inherited from his childhood: *"My worth depends on my success. Unless I'm better than others, I'm not good enough."* This belief became the invisible force driving him to constantly strive, compare, and compete with others.

When his career plateaued and his younger colleagues began to advance faster, Edmond's inner narrative turned against him. He thought, *"I'm losing my edge. Maybe I'm not as capable as I believed. What will people think if I don't succeed?"* These thoughts became obsessive and self-punishing. Each day he woke up with a knot of anxiety in his stomach, scrolling through his phone to see who was doing better, while secretly envying their success. The more he compared with others, the smaller he felt.

Emotionally, Edmond lived in a state of quiet despair - outwardly composed, yet inwardly fearful and empty. His self-esteem, built on the fragile foundation of external validation, began to collapse. He felt invisible without his achievements, as if his existence no longer mattered.

In therapy, we gently explored the roots of these beliefs. He began to see that his "need to prove himself" was not strength, but fear disguised as ambition - fear of not being loved or respected by others if he failed to succeed. As we examined his inner dialogue, Edmond noticed how often he used phrases like *"I must," "I should,"* and *"I can't fail."* These were the voice of his ego, not his true self.

Through mindfulness exercises and reflective journaling, Edmond gradually learned to observe his thoughts rather than believe them. He began replacing his self-critical thoughts such as *"I'm a failure"* with more grounded reflections: *"My worth doesn't depend on my job title or my professional achievements. I can contribute meaningfully to my family and my community in many other ways."*

Over time, his inner dialogue softened. The need to impress others faded and was gradually replaced by a quiet, grounded confidence. Edmond discovered peace in simply being, rather than constantly achieving. This shift marked the slow dissolution of his ego-based identity. He no longer saw himself as a lawyer striving to prove his worth, but as a human being expressing his true nature through his work. By letting go of the illusion that his career defined him, Edmond rediscovered the freedom and serenity of his authentic self.

As he reconnected with his deeper values - compassion, integrity, fairness, and kindness - Edmond realised that these qualities had always defined him, long before any professional accomplishment. He began volunteering his legal expertise to support disadvantaged families, and in doing so found a profound sense of fulfilment. Offering help, guidance, and hope to those in need - especially those without the financial means to access support - gave Edmond a true sense of meaning and purpose in his life.

Remember that the main obstacle to discovering your true essence is fear - the fear of losing your ego, or what you believe is your identity. You may feel afraid to move inward, listen to your heart, and discover your authentic self. But the truth is that the journey to self-realisation will begin only when you separate your ego (your false sense of identity) from your true self. For a deeper exploration of awakening beyond the ego and embodying your highest potential, I invite you to continue this transformative journey in the third book of my trilogy, *"Another Way of Living: How to Dissolve the Ego and Realise Your Divine Potential (Book 3)."*

Ego as Identification with the Mind

In essence, ego is identification with the mind. And the mind, due to its illusory nature, cannot see reality; it can only continue to believe in that which has been fed into it, in the past. Most people have allowed the mind to become their master, and that master now treats them as its servant.

When the mind becomes the master instead of the servant, it will dictate your life rather than serving your higher self. A mind that uses you, rather than being used by you, becomes destructive - to yourself and to others. Remember, you need to use your mind, but not to become identified with it. If you learn to use your mind properly, it will serve you well. For instance, you can use your mind as a powerful tool when you need to reflect, create something, or plan for the future. Use your mind - but remain above it!

Recognising that you are not the mind can help you become the master of your mind. Only when you stop identifying yourself with your mind and become egoless, your suffering will disappear. This inner shift will open the doorway to a deeper realisation: understanding what you truly are is the most important goal in life. For this reason, it becomes essential to release your attachment to the false self, dissolve the ego, and reconnect with your true essence.

Pathways to Dissolving the Ego

There are two main ways to dissolve the ego: meditation and love. Each works in a different yet complementary way - meditation through awareness, and love through connection.

Meditation will help you to become the silent observer of your mind. When you meditate, you begin to notice how thoughts and desires arise and pass away like clouds drifting across the sky. You start to see that you are not the thought, nor the thinker - you are the awareness behind both.

As this awareness deepens, you begin to recognise how easily the mind clings to its own creations. If you have a strong ego, it simply means that you are giving too much importance to your thoughts and desires. When a thought appears, you immediately identify with it; when a desire arises, you believe it defines who you are. To dissolve the ego, begin by observing these mental movements without engaging with them. Allow them to come and go - without judgement and without attachment. This is the shift from constant mental activity to pure awareness.

Once you begin to master your thoughts in this way, you can deepen the inner transformation by going beyond thinking altogether. One of the most natural ways to do this is by connecting with nature daily. Sit silently under a clear blue sky and meditate on its openness. Remain silent, and enter its clarity. Allow the clarity of the sky to enter deeply within you. Then, gradually, become the clarity. If you meditate long enough on an open, clear sky, soon you will notice that your thoughts will cease, and your mind will become silent.

In essence, to dissolve the ego, you need to move from your mind to your heart. Remember that the only way from your mind to your heart is to think less, and to feel more. The reasoning here is that whenever you are absorbed in the process of thinking, you create boundaries around yourself. In this way, you remain separate from others.

Hence, to begin your journey from the mind to the heart, you need to increase your sensitivity by quieting your mind, deepening your feelings, and experiencing them fully. To deepen your feelings, savour the taste of the food you eat, feel the coolness and freshness of the water you drink, and sense deeply the touch of your partner... When you connect with your heart through your feelings, you begin to dissolve the self-created boundaries around yourself. In this state of openness, you can more easily connect both with yourself and with others.

When you dissolve your ego and start living in your heart, you will be able to love, to share, and to give unconditionally. Remember, whenever you give from the heart, you want to give more. Whenever you think from the mind, you want to take more. The mind cannot trust, cannot love, and cannot give. It can only fear, criticise, and doubt. The more you live in your mind, the less capable you are of loving. The more you live in your heart, the more loving you are. The more loving you are, the more you act out of love. And the more you act out of love, the more you become who you truly are. When you slow down and become more thoughtless, you open a space for the heart to guide you back to the essence of your being. In this space, even the smallest moments become rich with presence and connection.

To illustrate this, let's look at a real-life example. My friend, Charlotte, a 46-year-old general practitioner, spent most of her life living in her head - constantly analysing, planning, and worrying. Her mind was always busy, filled with thoughts about her patients, her family, and the endless responsibilities waiting for her each day. Though deeply caring by nature, she often felt emotionally distant - unable to truly rest or to feel the warmth of her own heart.

When she began practising mindful eating and daily gratitude rituals, something subtle began to shift within her. Each morning, before rushing to work, Charlotte took a few quiet moments to breathe and write down three things she was grateful for - a warm cup of tea, her daughter's laughter, or the supportive words of a colleague. As she wrote, she didn't just think of gratitude - she felt it. She allowed the emotion to fill her chest like sunlight spreading through a dark room.

In the evenings, she ended her day by recalling one simple moment that had brought her joy - the softness of her child's hug, the golden glow of the sunset on her way home, or a kind word from a patient. Instead of rushing past these moments, she paused to let them echo within her heart. Slowly, her awareness began to descend from the mind's chatter into the quiet rhythm of her heart.

Charlotte also began expressing her gratitude aloud to her children, saying things like, *"I'm so grateful for the time we spent together today."* Each expression deepened her connection, softening the invisible walls she had built through years of mental overactivity. The more she spoke from her heart, the more her children responded with openness and affection.

Over time, she noticed a profound change. The anxious thoughts that once dominated her mind began to lose their grip. Her days no longer felt like an endless race against time but like a series of meaningful moments to be savoured and shared.

Through these simple practices, she rediscovered the joy of being - of feeling alive, connected, and at peace.

Charlotte's journey reminds us that the path from the mind to the heart does not require dramatic change - only gentle awareness and presence. By slowing down, feeling deeply, and allowing gratitude to awaken the heart, you dissolve the walls of separation and return to the natural state of love that has always been within you.

Here are a few simple gratitude rituals you can begin today to help you connect with your heart:

1. Morning Gratitude Ritual - Set the Tone for a Beautiful Day

Each new morning is a fresh beginning - a chance to start your day with appreciation rather than rush or distraction.

- Before reaching for your phone or thinking about what lies ahead, pause. Take a slow, conscious breath and write down three things you are truly grateful for. They can be as simple as a warm cup of tea, the sound of birds, or waking up with someone you love nearby.

- With each item, close your eyes and breathe gratitude into your heart. Feel it expanding through your chest, gently lifting your mood and setting a peaceful tone for the day.

Remember, when you start your morning with gratitude, you step into the day with clarity, calmness, and inner strength.

2. Evening Gratitude Ritual - Reflect, Appreciate, and Release

The end of the day invites you to slow down and recognise the hidden blessings that often go unnoticed.

- Before going to bed, recall one meaningful moment that made you smile or feel at peace - a kind word, a moment of laughter, a quiet walk, or something you accomplished. Relive that moment in your mind, feel it deeply, and let it warm your heart.

- Then, silently repeat: *"Thank you for this amazing day, for all that it taught me, and for the beautiful gifts it brought me."*

As you drift into rest, let go of any tension or regret, trusting that each day - even the challenging ones - carries something valuable for your growth.

3. Spontaneous Gratitude - Speak It, Share It, Live It

Gratitude grows stronger when it is expressed.

- Whenever you notice something beautiful - sunlight through the trees, a kind gesture, or a smile from a stranger - say it out loud or in your heart. For example, you may say: *"I am so grateful for this delicious meal,"* or *"Thank you for making me laugh today."* These simple words create ripples of positivity. They lift your energy and remind those around you of the goodness that exists in everyday moments.

When practised daily, these rituals gradually shift your focus from lack to abundance, from fear to appreciation. Gratitude becomes your quiet strength - dissolving ego-driven thoughts, anchoring you in the present moment, and opening your heart to life as it truly is: a continuous flow of blessings waiting to be noticed.

Surrender

When the exhausted night
Quietly gives away
To the glorious sunset,
That takes up the scene with full power
- It does surrender.

When the last winter days are nearly finished,
Unable to contain the upcoming spring,
They become warmer and warmer
To the pleasure of the living and the non-living
- They do surrender.

When the chattering mind
Finds the place of no thoughts,
Where silence replaces the loudness
And inner realms awaken,
- It does surrender.

So, surrender to the swirling wind
As light as a feather,
With no resistance and no questions...
Just drop your guard and fear not,
Because there is nothing to be afraid of.

When you surrender fully,
You are perfectly safe,
Because the Universe is all around you.
And there's nothing between you and God,
So, you unite again.

Making Right
Choices in Life

"All you have to do is decide moment by moment which voice you listen to: the truth of love or the nightmare of fear."
- Dragos Bratasanu

Q: How can we make right choices in life?

A: Many people struggle to make the right choices, and as a result, they often find themselves on the wrong path - a path filled with failure, disappointment, and unnecessary suffering. This happens most often when decisions are driven by fear: fear of failure, fear of insecurity, fear of not belonging, or fear of losing an important relationship.

When fear and doubt dominate your inner world, your judgement becomes clouded. You cannot make a clear, aligned choice when you are anxious, fearful, or confused. Fear narrows your perception, making you focus on what could go wrong rather than what is truly right for you. If you continue to make decisions based on fear, you will find yourself trapped in a cycle of misery and missed opportunities.

The reality is that you have an inner guide that can guide you to make the right decisions in life, but you may not know how to use it. Hence the important question is: "*How can you connect with your inner guide and follow it?*" Self-knowledge and self-awareness are crucial steps towards accessing your intuitive guidance.

To connect with your inner guide, it is essential to spend time alone every day for at least thirty minutes - preferably in nature. In solitude, you can connect deeply with your true self, and get to know your deepest values, preferences, and priorities. Alone in silence, you may ask yourself the following questions:

- *"What makes me truly happy?"*
- *"What brings joy into my life?"*
- *"What things will I no longer accept or tolerate in my life?"*

Then, listen attentively to what your heart is telling you. Importantly, once you become aware of something that is not right in your life, know that you can make a new, healthier choice. These new choices can lead to new and positive experiences in your life. These positive experiences in turn will bring positive changes in your life. As Heraclitus said wisely, *"Day by day, what you choose, what you think, what you do is who you become."*

Whenever you need to make an important decision in your busy life, try to make a conscious effort to stop the daily activities that you are engaged in throughout the day, and ask for inner guidance. Remember that essentially, wisdom comes from the inner depth of the human being. Hence, when you are faced with a dilemma or a problem to solve, you need to stop thinking about it and allow your intuition to guide you to make the right decision.

One person who discovered the power of intuition is Jordan. Jordan, a 45-year-old kindergarten teacher, had spent two decades in a secure but uninspiring job. Though he loved teaching, he longed to create something more personal and meaningful - a community learning centre where children could explore creativity, curiosity, and connection. Yet each time he considered leaving his stable position, fear gripped him. His mind raced with anxious thoughts: *"What if it fails?" "What if I can't support my family?" "What if I regret this decision?"*

In counselling, we created a reflective practice designed to quiet his overactive mind and connect him with his inner wisdom. Each evening, Jordan devoted 20 to 30 minutes for stillness. He would sit quietly, breathe deeply, and let his thoughts settle. Then, he would ask himself these simple but powerful questions: *"What is my heart trying to tell me?" "What would I regret more - staying safe or following my calling?"*

At first, he felt only confusion. But over time, as he kept listening inwardly, a new clarity began to emerge. One Saturday, while walking through a local community hall, Jordan stopped for a moment and imagined it alive with the sounds of children laughing and learning. He could almost feel the joy in that imagined space - a reflection of the joy within himself. In that moment, he felt a quiet bliss stirring within - a knowing beyond words: *"This is what I'm meant to do."*

From that day on, Jordan's choices came not from fear, but from trust. He began planning his learning centre while still teaching, taking one practical step at a time. As his vision unfolded, so did his confidence. When he finally left his job, it was not an act of escape, but a peaceful step towards a dream his soul had long held.

The following year, his community learning centre opened its doors. Soon it was filled with laughter, creativity, and gratitude. Watching children learn and thrive under his guidance, Jordan often reflected that the moment of clarity had not come from analysis or logic, but from silence - from listening deeply to the quiet voice within.

Jordan's experience illustrates how intuition emerges when the mind grows quiet and the heart opens. This inner wisdom is available to everyone - it simply requires awareness and presence. It speaks in whispers, not words - guiding us when we learn to listen in stillness.

To connect with your inner guide, you need to turn all your attention to the centre of your Being and reach the place where your inner peace resides. Once you are intrinsically connected with the deepest layers of your Being, you can clearly hear the answer to your question or dilemma. The answer will come to you through your intuition. Sometimes it might come through a remark from someone, a sentence from a book, or a chance encounter with a person. At other times, the response will come in form of a thought or an image in the mind, or in form of a feeling. Occasionally, it will appear in a dream, or through an experience that will occur throughout the day.

If you are deeply connected with yourself, you may receive the message even through the breeze of the wind, the songs of the birds, or the whisper of the river. The message will certainly come to you if you listen attentively. All you need to do is to connect with yourself deeply, and hear the whisper of the spirit, which is your intuition. Once you get the response aligned with your intuition, you need to make a decision, and then act accordingly.

If you want to deepen this connection and strengthen your intuitive guidance, you can try a scientifically grounded meditation technique I developed, called *"How to Open Your Third Eye and Connect with Your Higher Self."* It is available on my YouTube Channel, *Dr Snezhana*. By opening your third eye - the spiritual centre of intuitive knowledge - you can receive clear insights, cultivate open-mindedness, and strengthen your connection to your inner wisdom. This guided meditation technique is designed to help you quiet the mind, tune into your heart, and receive guidance that aligns with your higher self.

When you allow your inner guide to guide you, and receive the answer to your question, you will feel warmth, joy, enthusiasm, and love emanating from within. Then you will know that your inner guide has come into function. Once you begin to trust your inner guide and use it daily, you will begin to feel good within yourself and about yourself, as you will make choices and decisions that are beneficial for you. If you make choices that are good for you and your immediate surroundings, you will engage in more pleasant, life-supporting experiences. As you begin to produce such life experiences, everyone around you will feel the warmth in your presence as your whole being will vibrate with joy, peace, and love.

In essence, the path to wise decision-making is not about following external advice blindly – it is about learning to pause, connect deeply with yourself, and let your inner guide illuminate the right way for you. Remember that each conscious choice is an opportunity to shape a life filled with purpose, joy, and love.

The following practice will guide you to access that inner wisdom and make choices that feel true to your heart.

Practical Exercise: How to Connect with Your Inner Guide and Make Right Choices

Purpose: This exercise will help you to pause, connect with your inner self, and make decisions aligned with your intrinsic values.

Step 1: Create a Quiet Space

- Find a quiet place where you will not be disturbed for 15–30 minutes.

- Preferably, choose a natural setting (garden, park, by a river, or even a quiet room with soft lighting).

- Sit comfortably, and take 3-5 slow, deep breaths to calm your mind.

Step 2: Identify the Dilemma

- Write down the dilemma you are facing. Be as specific as possible.

- Example: *"Should I apply for this new job opportunity?"* or *"Should I end a friendship that feels draining?"*

Step 3: Recognise Your Fears

- Ask yourself: *"What fears, doubts, or pressures are influencing me?"*

- Write down any thoughts that create feelings of fear, doubt, insecurity, or pressure from others.

- Example: *"I'm afraid I'll fail,"* or *"I'm afraid I'll be judged by my colleagues."*

Step 4: Connect with Your True Values

- Ask yourself: *"What is truly important to me in this situation? What aligns with my core values?"*

- Write down what you truly want.

- Example: *"I value personal growth, creativity, and inner peace more than avoiding criticism."*

Step 5: Visualise the Outcomes

- Close your eyes and imagine each choice. How does it feel in your body, mind, and heart?

- Pay attention to your gut feelings - your intuition or any subtle feeling of excitement, or unease.

- Example: When imagining applying for the job, you might feel excitement and motivation; when imagining staying in your current role, you might feel stagnation or boredom.

Step 6: Listen to Your Inner Guide

- Sit in silence for a few minutes and ask: *"What is the wisest choice for me? What feels right to do?"*

- Be open to any answer that arises - through your thoughts, images, feelings, or even memories.

- Trust your first intuitive impression. And remember that your inner guide speaks in subtle whispers, not loud commands.

Step 7: Make a Decision and Take an Inspired Action

- Write down the decision you feel is best aligned with your values and intuition.

- Break it into small, actionable steps.

- Example: *"Step 1: Update my resume. Step 2: Research the company. Step 3: Submit my application."*

- Commit to taking the first step today.

Step 8: Reflect and Adjust

- After taking an inspired action, notice how you feel emotionally and physically. If you feel peace, joy, or enthusiasm, it is a sign that you made the right decision.

- Use these feelings as guidance to continue on your path, and adjust your actions as needed to stay aligned with your true self.

With regular practice, you will deepen your connection to your inner guide, allowing you to make right decisions with clarity and confidence. In this way, you will create a life filled with greater joy, purpose, and positive experiences.

But above all, remember this: Your inner guide is not something outside of you - it is the most authentic, wise, and untouched part of who you are. It has been quietly accompanying you through every challenge and every crossroads, waiting for the moment you finally choose to trust it.

When you learn to listen to this gentle inner voice and follow its guidance, you will no longer walk through life in confusion or fear. You will walk with certainty, with alignment, and with peace. Then, every choice you make becomes a step towards the person you were meant to be. And when you begin to trust your inner guide, life opens before you in a new way - paths become clearer, opportunities shine brighter, and even difficult moments begin to feel purposeful. This is the real secret to making right choices in life: Trust the wisdom within you. It will never lead you astray.

Maintaining Optimal Physical Health

"The greatest wealth is health."
- Virgil

Q: How can we improve our overall physical health and wellbeing?

A: To nurture our physical being, each of us needs to learn to live in tune with nature's daily cycles. Across cultures and throughout time, traditional societies have recognised that humans are intrinsically connected to the rhythms of the sun and the moon. Living in harmony with these natural cycles is fundamental to optimal health and wellbeing.

This understanding is supported by recent research on the healthiest, happiest, and longest-living populations in the world - including those in Okinawa (Japan), Sardinia (Italy), Nicoya (Costa Rica), Ikaria (Greece), and Loma Linda (California) - where people are more than twice as likely to reach the age of 90. Remarkably, these individuals not only live long but remain vibrant and healthy throughout their lives. They stay active without external help or support, engaging in gardening, dancing, socialising, and regular exercise. They nourish themselves with wholesome foods, live with purpose, and maintain a sense of vitality and independence well into advanced age.

What these thriving communities teach us is that true vitality comes from living in rhythm with the natural cycles of life. They teach us that each moment of the day offers an opportunity to restore balance, nurture inner harmony, and connect more deeply with ourselves and the world around us.

To live in alignment with these natural rhythms, let us explore the flow of a balanced day - from the awakening energy of the morning to the quiet stillness of the night - and discover how each cycle supports our body, mind, and spirit in its own unique way. Drawing on both contemporary research and the lived wisdom of the world's healthiest and happiest populations, this chapter reveals how attuning yourself to these daily cycles can enhance your vitality, resilience, and overall wellbeing.

The Morning Cycle (6:00 a.m. - 10:00 a.m.)

The morning cycle is a sacred window to awaken our body, lift our spirit, and greet the day with joy. The early hours of the day, especially between 6:00 a.m. and 8:00 a.m. are ideal for physical activity. Engaging in gentle exercise or mindful activity during this time - whether it's stretching, walking, dancing, or breathing exercises - not only stimulates our metabolism but also promotes increased energy, mental clarity, and a positive outlook on life.

Importantly, we need to choose physical activity that feels enjoyable and suits our nature. The reasoning here is that whatever feelings we experience during the chosen activity produces a corresponding vibration in our body while we do it. Hence, if the exercise is stressful, or involves strain, it will cause emotional stress in our body. And this unpleasant experience associated with the exercise will destroy our motivation to repeat it again. Therefore, any physical activity that we choose to do should be associated with pleasure, flow, and joy.

As the sun is still gentle in the early morning hours, the digestive fire within our body needed to process the food is also relatively weak. This is why the healthiest and longest-living populations in the world suggest that humans don't need a large meal first thing in the morning.

Contrary to popular belief, the first meal of the day shouldn't be the heaviest or the most important one. The reason is that if we eat while our digestive fire is still weak, the food won't be digested properly. Consequently, it is more likely to accumulate in the tissues of our body as fat and cause weight gain or obesity. Therefore, we should have breakfast as a light meal in the morning. For example, my breakfast usually consists of fresh fruit, a small serving of nuts, or a smoothie, which leaves me feeling light and nourished.

The Lunchtime Cycle (10:00 a.m. - 2:00 p.m.)

At this time of the day the strength of the sun is the strongest, and so is our body's digestive power. Naturally, this is the time when humans are designed to have the most substantial meal of the day - the lunch. Although it is suggested that lunch should be the main meal of the day, this does not necessarily mean that it should be a big meal.

To consume the right amount of food during the lunchtime cycle, we need to remember to listen to our body's internal messages and honour our appetite. For lunch, I personally make a balanced meal of proteins, vegetables, and whole grains. For example, I often enjoy grilled salmon or lentil patties served with a colourful salad of mixed greens, avocado, cherry tomatoes, and a drizzle of olive oil, along with a small portion of quinoa or brown rice. This combination fuels me for the rest of the day without making me feel sluggish. Following this practice has not only improved my digestion but also enhanced my mental clarity and overall energy levels in the afternoon.

The Afternoon Cycle (2:00 p.m. - 6:00 p.m.)

At this time of the day the energy level is relatively lower, and it is a time to re-energise the body. Thus, if we take 20 -30 minute - power nap or a brief rest at this time of the day, we can revitalise our energy. This in turn will enhance our alertness, strengthen the clarity of our mind, and boost our productivity.

After this short period of rest, it is good to have an afternoon tea such as healthy juice, tea, fruits, or some nuts. After the afternoon tea - if time and circumstances allow - it is good to engage in some pleasurable physical activity.

At this time of the day, after my power nap, I like to enjoy a light afternoon snack of fresh fruit, nuts, or herbal tea, which helps me maintain steady energy. Afterwards, I often take a short walk or spend a few minutes dancing, which re-energises me and keeps my motivation and focus high for the rest of the day.

The Evening Cycle (6:00 p.m. - 10:00 p.m.)

As the sun sets in the evening and its power is weak, the digestive fire of the human body is also weak. Therefore, if we have a large meal for dinner, the food won't be digested properly. This undigested food, over time will begin to interfere with the functioning of the organs of our body, resulting in impaired circulation, arteriosclerosis, weight gain, lethargy, and other physical or mental disturbances. Hence, we should aim to have a light meal at evening, ideally between 6.00 p.m. and 8.00 p.m. to allow sufficient time for the food to be digested properly.

After dinner, we can engage in some light and relaxing activities that help our mind, body, and soul prepare for sleep - such as a gentle walk, having an enjoyable conversation, watching a light TV show, reading a book, or meditating. These kinds of activities will help us calm down, and allow us to tune in with the first signs of sleep that usually occur around 10.00 p.m.

I personally enjoy a short walk with my husband, listening to smooth jazz music, reading a book, or meditating - simple pleasures that help me unwind peacefully. These small habits have improved the quality of my sleep and my overall sense of relaxation and wellbeing.

The Night Cycle (10:00 p.m. - 6:00 a.m.)

This is the time when the body eliminates toxins, repairs cells, and rejuvenates the entire system. To optimise its total rejuvenation, this is the ideal time when we need to be asleep. Remember, if you skip this crucial period for revitalisation of the body, your body won't be able to repair the cells, eliminate the toxins and revitalise the organs effectively. Therefore, it is essential to get uninterrupted sleep for eight hours, ideally from 10.00 p.m. till 6.00 a.m.

Living in Tune with Nature's Cycles

Taking steps today to align with nature's daily rhythms can make a profound difference in your life. In fact, modern science shows that this principle is reflected within us - our very cells are constantly regenerating and renewing:

- Stomach lining cells renew every five days.

- Liver cells regenerate over 300 -500 days.

- Red blood cells live for approximately four months.

- Brain cells replace themselves roughly every two months.

- The entire skeleton renews over ten years.

This means the way you take care of yourself today will impact how you will live your life tomorrow. By respecting the natural cycles - moving your body joyfully, eating mindfully, resting appropriately, and sleeping deeply - you can cultivate optimal health, lasting happiness, and sustainable energy.

From my own experience, I can confidently say that applying these practices has transformed my life. I feel healthier, more vibrant, and more energised each day. My mornings are full of clarity, my afternoons are productive and joyful, and my evenings are calm and restorative. Aligning with nature has not only enhanced my physical health but has also deepened my sense of wellbeing and contentment.

To help you align more closely with these natural rhythms, I've created a simple daily schedule based on both ancient wisdom and modern research. This structure serves as a gentle guide - one that you can adapt to your personal lifestyle while supporting your body's natural cycles of energy, rest, and renewal.

Daily Schedule for Optimal Health & Wellbeing

Morning Cycle (6:00 a.m. - 10:00 a.m.)

- **6:00 - 7:00 a.m.:** Begin your day with gentle physical activity - walking, yoga, stretching, or any light exercise you enjoy, followed by meditation and positive affirmations.

- **7:00 - 7:30 a.m.:** Prepare your breakfast.

- **7:30 - 8:00 a.m.:** Enjoy a light, nourishing breakfast such as fruit, a smoothie, nuts, or a small balanced meal.

- **8:00 - 9:00 a.m.:** Spend time in mindful planning, journaling, preparing for your day with calm focus, or using your commute as a moment for quiet reflection rather than stress.

- **9:00 - 10:00 a.m.:** *"The Golden Hour for Productivity"* - dedicate this time to your most important or creative work. With your mind clear, your body energised, and your focus sharp, you will set a positive tone for the rest of the day.

Lunchtime Cycle (10:00 a.m. - 2:00 p.m.)

- **10.00 - 10.30 p.m.**: Pause for a short mid-morning break: enjoy a cup of tea or coffee and allow your mind to recharge.

- **10.30 - 11.30 p.m.:** Ideal time for focused intellectual work, creative thinking, or engaging in a stimulating hobby.

- **11.30 - 12.00 p.m.:** Begin preparing lunch or winding down your morning tasks.

- **12:00 - 1:00 p.m.:** Have your main meal of the day. Aim for balanced, nutritious food while eating mindfully.

- **1:00 - 2:00 p.m.:** Take a light walk or

stretch to support your digestion and refresh your energy for the afternoon. If you prefer, you can also continue with your work or tasks, keeping a mindful pace to stay focused and calm.

Afternoon Cycle (2:00 p.m. - 6:00 p.m.)

- **2:00 - 2.30 p.m.:** Take a short rest or power nap to recharge your energy.

- **2:30 - 3.00 p.m.:** Take a gentle pause, repeat positive affirmations, and begin preparing your afternoon snack.

- **3:00 - 3.30 p.m.:** Enjoy your nourishing snack - such as fresh fruit, tea, nuts, or a natural juice - while allowing your body and mind to reset for the rest of the day.

- **3.30 - 4.30 p.m.:** Complete important tasks at work, focusing on productivity and efficiency, or engage in creative and expressive activities such as writing, painting, drawing, or any fulfilling hobby that nourishes your mind and spirit.

- **4.30 - 5.00 p.m.:** Wrap up your workday, tie up loose ends, and prepare for a smooth transition out of the office.

- **5.00 - 5.30 p.m.:** Commute home mindfully, using this time to relax, reflect on your day, or listen to uplifting music or an inspiring podcast.

- **5.30 - 6.00 p.m.:** Prepare for your dinner.

Evening Cycle (6:00 p.m. - 10:00 p.m.)

- **6:00 - 7:00 p.m.:** Have a light, easily digestible dinner, such as soup, salad, or steamed vegetables.

- **7:00 - 8:00 p.m.:** Engage in a pleasurable physical activity (walking, gardening, stretching, or dancing) or sharing pleasant conversation.

- **8:00 - 9:00 p.m.:** Begin winding down - read, watch a light TV show, or listen to calming music.

- **9:00 - 9:30 p.m.:** Prepare for sleep. Spend a few minutes in meditation, gratitude practice, or prayer to calm your mind and nurture your spirit. Keep your bedroom dark and cool, allowing your body to naturally repair and rejuvenate.

- **Night Cycle (10:00 p.m. - 6:00 a.m.)**

- **10:00 p.m.:** Sleep for 8 uninterrupted hours.

By aligning your sleep with nature's cycle of darkness and light, you awaken restored - ready to greet a new day in harmony with yourself and the world around you.

How to Use This Template

- **Fill in your preferred activities in each block.**

- Use this template as a flexible guide. Include the activities that bring you joy, focus, and balance - whether it's work tasks, creative pursuits, exercise, or moments of rest and reflection. Personalising it will make it easier to follow and more rewarding.

- **Adapt times slightly to suit your personal schedule but try to honour the natural cycles.**

- Everyone's day is unique, so shift the timing of activities to fit your life. However, wherever possible, align your tasks with the natural rhythms of the day - morning energy, midday focus, afternoon refreshment, and evening rest - for optimal wellbeing.

- **Track your energy, mood, and health for a few weeks to notice improvements.**

- Pay attention to how you feel physically, emotionally, and mentally throughout the day. Journaling or using a simple log can help you spot patterns, identify what energises or drains you, and see the benefits of living in tune with natural cycles over time.

- **Adjust your meals, exercise, and rest based on how your body responds.**

- This template is not one-size-fits-all. Listen to your body and make small tweaks as needed - shift mealtimes, change exercise intensity, or modify rest periods - so your daily rhythm supports your health, clarity, and vitality.

- **Be patient and consistent.**

- Developing harmony with natural cycles takes time. Give yourself grace, and focus on steady, mindful practice rather than perfection. With consistent effort, you will begin to notice improved energy, focus, and a deeper sense of balance in your daily life.

Remember, transformation begins with small, intentional steps. By embracing simple, consistent changes, like walking in the morning, having a light breakfast, or taking a short afternoon rest, you can strengthen the body, uplift the spirit, and empower the mind. When practised with awareness and consistency, these mindful actions can create profound and lasting changes in your physical, mental, and spiritual wellbeing.

Understanding the Mind-Body Connection

"The Mind is like the rider and the body is like the horse. [In other words, your mind can, like a rider directing a horse, learn to direct the body.]"
- A famous Buddhist saying

Q: How are the mind and the body connected?

A: Every thought or belief we hold about ourselves or our immediate environment impacts us. The reason is that every thought, feeling and action we give birth to produces a corresponding energy of vibration. Hence, if our thoughts, feelings and actions are positive and life-supporting, the corresponding ripples that return to us and our physical wellbeing will be positive and life-supporting. In contrast, if we have predominantly stressful thoughts and feelings throughout the day, they will have an adverse effect on us, and our physical body.

Modern science confirms what ancient wisdom has long taught: our mental and physical health are deeply intertwined. Dr Sheldon Cohen, a psychologist at Carnegie Mellon University[1], conducted groundbreaking research showing that chronic emotional stress weakens the immune system's ability to regulate its inflammatory response. In turn, those who experienced prolonged stress were more likely to develop many inflammatory diseases including cold, asthma, autoimmune disorders, and heart problems.

Negative feelings, if not managed effectively, may significantly affect the functioning of the organs in our body. For example, anxious feelings are accompanied by odd physical sensations deep in the gut, known as "butterflies in the stomach." Suppressed anger can directly affect the functioning of the liver, blocking the liver's energy flow, while fear can interfere with the functioning of the bladder. Conversely, when we are joyful, our hearts not only feel joy emotionally but also experience it

---

1 *Sheldon Cohen et al. 2012, "Chronic stress, glucocorticoid-receptor resistance, inflammation, and disease risk," Psychological and Cognitive Sciences, vol.109, pp. 5995-5999.*

physically. Hence, the happier we feel, the healthier our cells are.

Happy thoughts = happy feelings = a healthy body.

Stressed thoughts = upsetting feelings = a body in dis-ease.

Therefore, the greatest thing you can do for your physical health and emotional wellbeing is to learn how to control your mind. As Louise Hay, the beloved American inspirational teacher, once said: *"The only thing you ever have control over is your current thought."* Once you learn to control your mind, soon you will realise that you are not a victim of your negative thoughts and limiting beliefs, but rather a master of your mind.

How to Control Your Mind

Here are some practical ways of how you can learn to control your mind:

1. Discover Gaps in the Stream of Thinking

Create inner space in your mind by paying attention on the gaps between your thoughts. These moments don't need to be long - even a few seconds scattered throughout your day will begin to transform your state of mind. What matters more than their duration is their frequency. By inviting these moments of stillness regularly, your daily activities and stream of thinking will become interspersed with space. In this way, you will conserve more mental energy that you may use towards expressing your creativity and unlocking your full potential.

As Eckhart Tolle explained, *"Without those gaps, your thinking becomes repetitive, uninspired, devoid of any creative spark."* In those gaps some great ideas may arise. In fact, this is how the greatest mathematician of all ages, Albert Einstein discovered the theory of relativity - while playing with soap bubbles in his bath.

2. Embrace the Power of Positive Affirmations

Begin and end your day with uplifting affirmations. Writing or speaking positive statements about yourself and your life will raise your energy, strengthen your willpower, and increase your faith. The most powerful times to practise your positive affirmations are in the stillness of the morning, just after waking, and at night before you go to sleep, when your mind is especially receptive.

Before starting to affirm, ensure that your mind is calm and free from worries, or any mental discomfort. Then, choose one positive affirmation that addresses your most pressing need, and evokes a sense of power and inspiration within you. At first, repeat your chosen affirmation loudly and slowly few times - with devotion, faith and sincerity - then softer, until your voice becomes a whisper. Then, continue to affirm it several times mentally (in your mind only), without even moving your lips. If you do it properly, by focusing all your attention on each word, you will begin to feel a great sense of joy and serenity within. In this way, you will allow the chosen affirmation to penetrate your subconsciousness and return with unlimited power to fulfil your desire in the material world.

Here is a collection of my favourite positive affirmations, which can inspire positive changes in your life.

Love Affirmations

- ✓ I allow love to fill every part of my body, and I radiate it outward.
- ✓ I am willing to love and accept myself exactly as I am.
- ✓ Loving myself fills my heart, mind, and soul with peace and joy.

- ✓ I show myself love, kindness and respect every day.
- ✓ I am a unique and valuable gift to the world.
- ✓ Life loves me, and I love life.

Health Affirmations

- ✓ Every cell in my body radiates health.
- ✓ I have abundant energy throughout the day.
- ✓ I express my joy freely through singing and dancing.
- ✓ My body is perfect just as it is.
- ✓ I nourish my body with healthy food and drinks.
- ✓ I treat my body with warmth, tenderness and compassion.
- ✓ I have a healthy and slender body.
- ✓ I love my body unconditionally.

Affirmations for Finding a Fulfilling Job

- ✓ I am ready and deserving of a wonderful new job where I can use my talents, skills, and creativity in ways that bring me deep fulfilment and joy.

- ✓ I trust that the right opportunities come to me at the right time.
- ✓ I am guided to the perfect job that nurtures my personal growth and career development.
- ✓ Each interview and application bring me closer to the job position that fits my highest potential.
- ✓ I attract work environments where I am valued, respected, and appreciated for who I truly am.
- ✓ I am grateful for the opportunity to do work that aligns with my passions, values, and purpose.
- ✓ The joy I find in my career is reflected in my overall happiness.

Success Affirmations

- ✓ The ground I am on is a successful ground.
- ✓ I have unlimited potential.
- ✓ Creative and innovative ideas come to me easily and effortlessly.
- ✓ My work brings me pleasure, satisfaction and financial abundance.

- ✓ My life is unfolding in alignment with my highest potential.
- ✓ I am a success story.

Wealth Affirmations

- ✓ I am an irresistible magnet for all that belongs to me by Divine right.
- ✓ My income is constantly increasing.
- ✓ I am rich and successful person who does good in the world.
- ✓ I use my money to create more joy in my life and in the lives of others.
- ✓ The more I give, the more I receive.
- ✓ I am abundant in every area of my life.
- ✓ I am financially free.

Empower yourself with these transformative affirmations to silence your self-judgement, dissolve your negative self-talk, and create a life filled with abundance, love, and purpose. Remember: each positive thought you choose, each empowering affirmation you speak- is a step towards becoming the fully radiant, unstoppable version of yourself that you were always meant to be!

I Wonder...

Where the Sun hides
When the Moon takes over?

And where the rainbow disappears
When the warmth dries the raindrops?

What happens to the wind
When it gets pushed away?

And where my thoughts reside
When my mind quietly rests?

What happens to my soul
When I leave my body?

And where has this minute gone
While I asked you these questions?

Tell me, do you know?

While I wait for your answers
What happened to my questions?

Increasing Self-Knowledge and Self-Understanding

"Self-knowledge is the beginning of wisdom.
Self-knowledge is cultivated through the
individual's search of himself."
- Jiddu Krishnamurti

Q: I believe that self-knowledge is the foundation of better living and genuine self-improvement. But how can we expand our self-knowledge?

A: The journey to truly know yourself is one of the most fascinating and rewarding paths you can walk. Yet to deepen your self-knowledge, you must first become familiar with the self itself - especially its mental and spiritual dimensions. To better understand these important aspects of the self, I will use the following metaphor that comes from the author of the book *"Mindfulness Prescription for Adult ADHD,"* Lidia Zylovska: *"Imagine that your mind is like a big, blue ocean, vast and deep. And just like there are always waves on the surface of the ocean, your thoughts can be restless, agitated, or choppy. Yet underneath, there is always calm water, no matter how restless the ocean's surface gets."*

This analogy can be applied to the mind and the spirit that are fundamental parts of each human being. Beneath the thoughts which always appear on the surface of the mind, there is an ocean of peace. If you dive deeply, you will discover that the peace you have been searching for outside of yourself has always been present deep within you.

It is important to understand that ordinarily, people can be engaged either in the process of thinking, or they can experience an inner state of pure existence, without any thoughts interfering. When people are engaged in the process of thinking, they usually become identified with their thoughts. By giving significance to their thoughts, they continually allow them to affect their inner emotional state. At the same time, they are overthrowing the value of their own Being. In this way, they allow to become victims of their negative thoughts and limiting beliefs, rather than masters of their own mind.

When the mind becomes devoid of any thought, people can attain a peaceful state of pure consciousness, and connect deeply with their inner Being. Remember that essentially, we are not "human doings", but we are Human Beings. Being is the source from which all thoughts, actions, and creativity arise. In order to think, we must first be. In order to do something, we must first exist. Hence, our Being is the basis of all our activities. Being is the source of life, and the source of all our inventiveness and creativity. Thus, to increase your self-knowledge, it is vital to become familiar with the nature of your Being.

In essence, Being is inherently unchanging in its absolute state of infinite bliss. As Human Beings, we were made to be joyful, peaceful, and blissful on a permanent basis. However, whenever you experience any object without paying attention to the state of your Being, you become identified with the object itself. Then, the impression of the object becomes strong in your mind. If that experience made a positive impression in your mind, you will have the desire to repeat the same experience again. Alternatively, you will feel compelled to go through the same thoughts related to that experience, over and over again. Therefore, most of us constantly chase pleasurable experiences in life in order to feel good. In this way, we unceasingly search for happiness outside ourselves - in the material world - which can provide only temporary relief and pleasure.

Yet there is another way of living - another way of Being. If you can keep your attention on your Being, and stay aware of the blissful state of your existence, you will begin to see that the thoughts and experiences passing through your mind are only temporary. Their transitory nature prevents them from leaving a deep impression on you. In this way, the fleeting nature of your thoughts or the external experiences cannot disturb your peace. By consciously staying connected to your natural state of Being, you will retain your inner peace, joy and bliss under all circumstances. Then, you can always feel good within yourself - while thinking, acting, and responding in harmony with the natural flow of life.

With regular practice, everyone can succeed in accessing the spiritual source within, and living it daily. From my personal experience, living in alignment with my Being is a state that cannot be fully described with words. In this state of mind each of us can access our highest creativity, our deepest intuitions, and our most profound joys. As Lama Surya Das wisely said, *"What we seek is not outside ourselves... It is so close, we overlook it."*

The following practical exercise is designed to help you cultivate a harmonious dance between your inner awareness and outer experience, so that even in the midst of thinking, acting, or feeling, your inner peace remains intact. With regular practice, this connection can transform your mind, and guide you into a life of greater ease, true joy, and authentic fulfillment.

Practical Exercise: Exploring Your Inner Ocean

Step 1: Create Your Space

Find a quiet, comfortable spot where you can sit undisturbed for 10-15 minutes. Close your eyes, relax your body, and take a few deep, grounding breaths. Let the world soften around you...

Step 2: Observe the Mind's Waves

Imagine your mind as a vast ocean... Notice the thoughts rising and falling on the surface like waves.

Don't try to stop them, judge them, or analyse them - simply observe them... Recognise that these waves are natural and temporary.

Step 3: Dive Into Inner Stillness

Now, gently shift your attention beneath the waves, towards the calm, deep waters of your inner Being. Feel the stillness that lies beneath the surface turbulence... Anchor your awareness in this serene depth for few minutes, letting it expand through your entire body, mind, and soul.

Step 4: Anchor Your Being in Your Daily Life

Gradually bring this awareness of inner calm into your present experience. Whether you are thinking, acting, or feeling, notice the waves without letting them disturb the stillness within yourself. Know that your Being is always present, as a peaceful witness to the ebb and flow of life.

Step 5: Reflect and Journal

After the practice, spend 5 minutes journaling. Note any insights, moments of clarity, or feelings of joy, peace, or creativity that arose when you connected yourself with your Being. Over time, these reflections will reveal how deeply your inner sanctuary is influencing your daily life.

Consider this exercise not as a task, but as a journey - a gentle return to the depths of your inner ocean. Each time you reconnect with this stillness, your bond with your true self deepens. Over time, you may begin to notice a quiet, yet profound transformation: a mind that flows with calm, a heart that opens more fully, and a life lived from the serene, blissful centre of your Being. By returning to this inner space regularly, you will awaken the door to extraordinary possibilities, embracing profound peace, limitless inspiration, and the full expression of your highest self.

Cultivating Mindfulness

"Minding the mind, one becomes mindful. Not minding the mind, one becomes mindless."
- Stonepeace

Q: What is mindfulness, and how can I integrate it into my daily life?

A: Mindfulness is a state of heightened awareness, of being fully in the present moment. It is a state of non-judgemental observation. More specifically, mindfulness is a state of present time awareness, without evaluating or criticising the things, people or events in life, but accepting and acknowledging them as they are. In this state, the mind does not get caught up in any thoughts or feelings about the past or the future, but just let them go.

You can integrate mindfulness into your daily life by becoming more aware of your thoughts, feelings, and actions in every moment of your day. You can do this by focusing all your undivided attention to what you are doing in the present moment. For example, when you are eating, you are paying full attention on the process of consuming the food, and nurturing the body. When you are reading, your focus is only on what you are reading, and so on.

Mindfulness can be illustrated in this way: If you are having a lunch in a restaurant while thinking about your current or future projects, or your home responsibilities, you are not really present in the moment. You are not really eating your lunch, so you cannot taste the real flavour of the food, and enjoy it fully. You are "eating" your projects, your concerns, and your responsibilities. In such situations, you need to get back to yourself, to the centre of your Being, free yourself from all your worries and problems, and produce your true presence. Then, you will genuinely enjoy the flavour of the food.

Through various mindfulness techniques, you can access this state of highly alert yet relaxed attention. Remember, when you learn to control your attention, you will learn to control your mind. Hence, to integrate mindfulness in your life, you may begin by focusing your full attention on your thoughts and feelings in the present moment. This is called *"Mindful Self-Observation"* (this technique is described below).

Mindful Self-Observation

As often as possible throughout the day, ask yourself:

- *"How do I feel right now?"*
- *"Why do I feel this way?"*
- *"What am I thinking at this moment?"*

The key is to begin the process of becoming more aware of your thoughts and feelings, and to start listening to your body's internal messages. Each time you notice unpleasant feelings, try to identify the negative thoughts behind them. Then, you may take a moment to pause, recognise that those thoughts are unhelpful, and release the negativity. Once you do that, you can consciously choose positive, life-supporting thoughts that will help you feel better immediately.

For example, when you wake up in the morning and you begin to feel stressed or annoyed, you might think: *"I have so many things to do this morning. How can I achieve everything? Oh, look at the clock. I'm going to be late. I don't have time for breakfast",* and so on. At that moment, stop, and take a few deep breaths. Become aware of the negative thoughts that are causing you distress, and then consciously replace them with thoughts that will generate more pleasant feelings.

To do this, you may ask yourself: *"What kind of day do I want to have today?"* This is a powerful question, as it can shift your focus towards predominantly positive thoughts. For example, this question might generate thoughts like these: *"I have some important tasks to accomplish today. I will do my best to complete them on time while enjoying the process. And I will also find some time throughout the day to recharge my energy. I believe that I will have a very productive and successful day."*

Remember, when you feel good inside, you will attract more positive experiences in life. This is the law of the nature. Once you learn to control your mind, and live attuned with the natural laws, you will realise that you are not victim of your previous negative thoughts, beliefs and experiences, but rather a master of your mind.

The practice of concentrating all your attention on a specific object is another way of focusing the mind. Hence, another technique that can help you improve your concentration, and enrich your experience of being in the present is called *"Mindful Observation of a Flower."* This simple but powerful technique involves simply looking at a flower with full attention, and remaining silent, with no thoughts interfering. When all your attention is focused on the flower, everything else from your world disappears. Then, only the experience of the flower remains in your consciousness. This experience can make you feel more relaxed, energised, and revitalised. When you focus your total attention inward, you will become more mindful of your own presence, and your inner world.

Below is an explanation of this technique. (Please read the description, and focus all your attention on the picture below.)

Mindful Observation of a Flower (Part One)

Focus all your attention on the rose. Observe its shape, the delicate curves of its petals, the richness of its colours, and the subtle texture of each layer. Allow your eyes to take in every detail, noticing what you may have overlooked before.

Now, imagine inhaling the scent of the rose, letting it fill your lungs as you breathe in through your nose. As you exhale slowly, visualise any tension, stress, or heaviness leaving your body with each breath. With each cycle of inhalation and exhalation, feel yourself becoming more present, calm, and connected to the simple beauty of this moment.

Once you master the first part of this technique, you may move on to the second part of this exercise. You can choose to do this with your eyes closed, if that helps you focus inwardly.

Mindful Observation of a Flower (Part Two)

Imagine that the rose is connected by a long, graceful stem to the centre of your Being, located in your heart area. The root of the rose represents this inner centre. Visualise yourself gently moving down the stem towards the root, feeling a subtle connection between the flower and your heart. Bring your full attention to the root of the rose. Observe it carefully, noticing its presence and the sense of life it embodies.

Now, feel the warmth radiating in your heart area. Inhale this sensation of warmth and peace, letting it fill your entire body with each breath... Stay with this feeling, allowing yourself to savour it fully. Let yourself immerse in the quiet joy and serenity that arises from this connection to your inner Being...

As you open your eyes, carry this sense of peace, warmth, and presence with you. Remember that this inner stillness is always accessible, no matter where you are or what you are doing.

Integrating Mindfulness Daily

Mindfulness deepens through gentle, consistent practice. Each time you pause to breathe consciously, observe your surroundings, or notice a thought passing through your mind, you are training your awareness to return home - to this very moment. Gradually, you will begin to step out of the automatic patterns shaped by fear, worry, or past pain. You will realise that presence itself is your sanctuary - a space untouched by the noise of the world.

Whenever you feel scattered, anxious, or overwhelmed, remember that you always have the power to come back - to your breath, to your body, to the here and now. With each return, your mind grows steadier, your heart softer, and your spirit clearer. As mindfulness becomes woven into the fabric of your daily life, something beautiful begins to unfold. You start to live more consciously - listening deeply, moving gently, speaking kindly, and meeting each moment as it comes. You reconnect with the essence of your Being, a quiet awareness that has always been there, patiently waiting beneath the surface of your thoughts.

From this awareness arises a subtle joy - not the fleeting joy of circumstances, but the serene joy of being alive. A deep peace blossoms from within, and you begin to experience life not as something to control or endure, but as something to embrace and celebrate. This is the heart of mindfulness: returning again and again to the present, where life, love, and freedom are always waiting for you.

In the Now

Perfect comes from perfect
Which is the now.

Nothing is more perfect
Then this moment alone.

Fear comes from the future,
Sadness comes from the past.

Both aren't or won't be perfect,
Neither yesterday nor tomorrow.

Love comes from love
Which can only be in the now.

Love is perfect, so love here and now
And you become perfect.

Listening Attentively

"We have two ears and one mouth so that we can listen twice as much as we speak."
- Epictetus

Q: What does it mean to listen attentively?

A: Attention is a state of silent alertness with no thoughts interfering. To listen attentively means to bring all our undivided attention to what has been said in the act of communication. It means to hear everything that the other person is saying - without filtering it through our own assumptions or interpretations.

Most people, however, struggle to listen attentively to others, as they continue to think when the other person is talking. Remember, if you are thinking about what has been said in the act of communication, you can hear only your own interpretation, not the other person's actual words. Hence, you will already have an opinion, answer, or conclusion, before anything is said.

By interpreting the message in your own way, you will actually change the meaning of the words, and therefore misinterpret the message. Inevitably, this will influence your response, and the outcome of the interaction. As Roy Benett declared:

"The greatest problem with communication is we don't listen to understand. We listen to reply. When we listen with curiosity, we don't listen with the intent to reply. We listen for what's behind the words."

In my book *"Another Way of Living: A Journey to Self-Realisation (Book 2),"* I take you on a transformative exploration of the most common negative thinking patterns - known in psychology as cognitive distortions - that often create misconceptions in our communication. Beyond raising awareness, this book provides practical strategies and empowering solutions to help you identify and overcome these unhelpful patterns, fostering clearer thinking, deeper understanding, and more harmonious connections with the people around you.

Yet understanding what it means to listen is only the beginning. The real transformation happens when we begin to practise this awareness in our daily interactions - when we allow presence to replace reaction, and curiosity to take the place of judgement. In that space of attentive stillness, something remarkable occurs: we begin not only to hear others but to truly understand them.

The following real-life story beautifully illustrates the transformative power of mindful listening. Claire, a 42-year-old housewife, arrived at my counselling session with a quiet but palpable frustration about her marriage. Her eyes were filled with tears as she said, *"My husband never really listens to me."* Beneath her words was a quiet ache - a longing to be heard, and understood.

When I invited her to reflect on their conversations, she began to notice a pattern: her husband would often interrupt, offering quick solutions or turning the focus back to his own experiences. *"It feels like my feelings are not important for him,"* she said softly. Then, with a moment of introspection, Claire realised that she, too, sometimes fell into the same pattern - especially with her children. In her eagerness to help, she would often finish their sentences or assume she already knew what they were going to say.

This insight opened a door within her. Through our sessions, Claire began practising mindful listening - pausing before responding, breathing through her urge to speak, and allowing silence to hold space for the other person's truth. At first, it felt uncomfortable - her mind wanted to rush in with answers. But as she learned to stay present, she began to truly hear.

Gradually, her conversations with her husband transformed. Her husband noticed Claire's calm attention and began mirroring her approach, speaking more gently, and listening with curiosity rather than defense. Within weeks, their exchanges softened. The tension that once clouded their evenings was replaced by warmth, laughter, and mutual respect.

Claire later described it beautifully: *"When I stopped speaking to be heard and started listening to understand, a new harmony began to grow between us."* In learning to listen fully without judgement, she not only deepened the relationship with her husband but also rediscovered the quiet joy of human connection. Through the simple art of listening attentively, love found its natural voice again.

The Transformative Power of Listening Attentively

In the act of communication, you need to make a conscious effort to still your inner voice, focus fully on the conversation, and listen carefully with all your senses. At the same time, you must remain open to receive others' opinions without any judgement, criticism, or condemnation. Most importantly, you need to "forget yourself totally", and focus solely on the words, feelings, and unspoken cues the other person is conveying. In this way, you will hear the message more accurately, and be able to respond appropriately.

If you listen attentively and with care, people will feel respected and valued in your presence. They will sense that you are giving them your time and attention, and that their concerns genuinely matter to you. Attentive listening allows you to better understand their message and respond with appropriate advice or information. At the same time, if you listen attentively to others' perspectives, you might get a new insight about the issue at hand, and that insight might transform you.

To help you deepen this skill and experience the power of true presence, try the following practice:

A Practical Exercise: The Art of Listening Attentively

Imagine a conversation where you are truly present, fully attentive, and open to everything the other person is expressing. In this space, listening goes beyond words - you sense the feelings, the intentions, the unspoken messages. By practising in this way, you learn to listen with your heart, understand more deeply, and cultivate the connections that bring richness and meaning to your life.

You may try this exercise with a partner, friend, colleague, or a family member:

1. Set aside five quiet minutes where one person speaks and the other only listens. Choose a calm space where you won't be interrupted.

2. The speaker can talk about anything - a moment from their day, a recent challenge, or something that feels meaningful right now.

3. The listener's role is to be fully present.

- Remain silent except for brief acknowledgements such as *"I see,"* or *"mm-hmm."*

- Maintain gentle eye contact and open, relaxed body language.

- Notice any urge to interrupt, advise, or share your own story - and simply let it pass.

- Focus all your attention on the speaker's words, tone, and emotions. Listen not only with your ears, but with your heart.

4. When the speaker finishes, reflect back what you heard - without judgement, correction, or interpretation. For example, you may say: *"I understand that you felt disappointed when things didn't turn out the way you hoped. Is that right?"*

5. Switch roles and repeat the process, allowing the listener to become the speaker.

6. Afterward, take a moment together to reflect. Notice how it felt to be listened to without interruption, and how it felt to listen without speaking. What emotions or insights arose? Did you feel calmer, closer, or more open?

This simple yet profound exercise can transform everyday conversations into moments of genuine connection. It softens defensiveness, deepens understanding, and reminds us that listening itself is an act of love.

Remember, true listening is an act of presence, a gift you offer to another human being. And in giving this gift, you often find that you receive something even greater: a deeper connection, a clearer perspective, and a deep transformation within yourself.

Communicating Effectively

"The way we communicate with others and with ourselves ultimately determines the quality of our lives."
- Tony Robbins

Q: What does it mean to communicate effectively?

A: In general, people tend to use one of four common styles of communication: passive, aggressive, passive-aggressive, or assertive. Each style reflects a unique set of underlying beliefs, emotional patterns, and habitual behaviours, which in turn influence how messages are conveyed and received. Recognising these communication styles - and the beliefs and emotional tendencies that shape them - can help you become more aware of your own patterns, manage conflicts more effectively, and enhance your ability to communicate with respect, understanding, and dignity.

Passive Communication Style

Silence and assumption are the hallmarks of the passive communication style. People who communicate passively disregard their own opinions, feelings, needs, and desires. They believe that other people's opinions are more important, so what they think or say - doesn't really matter. The main reason is that passive communicators often struggle with low self-esteem and a lack of self-respect, so they place others' needs and desires above their own. Thus, passivity takes away their power and allows others to decide the outcomes of situations.

Importantly, once these individuals reach their high tolerance limit for unacceptable behaviour, they are prone to explosive outbursts of anger, which are usually out of proportion to the triggering situation. After the outburst, they usually experience feelings of shame and guilt, so they return to being passive again.

Ways of speaking:

- *"I don't mind."*
- *"That's fine."*
- *"Yes, sure."*

Beliefs:

- *"You are okay. I'm not."*
- *"I can't stand up for my rights."*
- *"People never consider my feelings."*

Behaviour: Passive communicators usually avoid eye contact, look down, and implore mercy.

Consequences: These individuals give in to others, are self-critical, and fail to express openly and clearly their feelings, needs or opinions. Hence, they usually don't get what they want or need in life.

In my counselling practice, I once worked with Helen, a 34-year-old accountant, who illustrated this pattern vividly. Whenever I asked for her input, she would smile politely and say things like, *"Whatever you decide is fine,"* or *"I don't want to cause any trouble."* On the surface, Helen seemed easy-going and accommodating, but deep down she often felt invisible and unheard.

At work, Helen usually stayed silent during staff meetings, even when she had valuable ideas to contribute. Thoughts like, *"It's probably not that important,"* or *"Someone else will explain it better,"* would stop her from speaking up. Later, when her colleagues received recognition for ideas similar to her own, she felt a familiar mix of frustration and self-blame, wondering, *"Why didn't I just say something?"*

At home, she allowed her partner to make most decisions - from what they ate for dinner to how they spent their weekends. Although part of her longed to express her preferences, another part whispered, *"It's easier not to make a fuss,"* or *"If I disagree, he might get upset."* Over time, this quiet suppression built an invisible wall inside her - one made of resentment, sadness, and exhaustion.

One evening, after yet another situation where she felt dismissed, her suppressed emotions overflowed. She found herself shouting in anger over something trivial, surprising both her partner and herself. The outburst left her shaken and filled with guilt and shame. She confided later, *"I don't even know why I got so angry - I hate that I lost control."*

Through counselling, Helen began to uncover the deeper belief driving her passivity - the conviction that her needs and wishes were somehow less important than others'. With gentle practice, she started using small but powerful statements such as, *"I'd actually prefer to..."* or *"That doesn't work for me."* At first, these words felt uncomfortable, but over time they became natural expressions of self-respect.

As Helen grew more comfortable voicing her thoughts and feelings, subtle yet meaningful shifts began to unfold in her relationships. At work, when she started sharing her ideas in meetings, her colleagues began to listen with interest and appreciation. Her manager often asked for her input, and a few of her suggestions were later implemented. Instead of feeling invisible, Helen felt seen and valued for her contribution. This recognition, in turn, encouraged her to participate more actively, transforming her quiet compliance into confident collaboration.

At home, Helen's newfound honesty brought a different kind of closeness to her marriage. When she expressed her preferences - whether about dinner plans or weekend activities - her husband initially seemed surprised, but soon welcomed her openness. Conversations that once ended with polite agreement became moments of genuine exchange. They began to make decisions together, and Helen noticed a warmth returning to their relationship - a sense of partnership built on authenticity rather than avoidance.

With each step, Helen realised that asserting herself did not create conflict, but harmony. By valuing her own voice, she invited others to value it too - and for the first time in years, she felt both heard and connected, not only to others but also to herself.

Helen's story beautifully illustrates how the passive style, though often driven by kindness and a desire to keep peace, can silently erode one's self-worth and connection with others over time. True harmony arises not from avoiding conflict, but from expressing one's truth with honesty and respect.

Having explored the passive style, let's now turn to the opposite end of the communication spectrum - the aggressive communication style.

Aggressive Communication Style

Aggressive communication is a style in which individuals express their thoughts, feelings, or needs in a forceful way that disregards or violates the rights of others. Aggressive communicators can be demanding, manipulative, or harsh. Instead of seeking harmony and mutual respect, these individuals strive for control and dominance, often at the expense of others' feelings, needs, and rights. They often interrupt, blame, or dominate conversations, believing that they are always right while others are always wrong. Sometimes this can compromise even the safety of others as well, as they can be verbally and/or physically abusive. This communication style often generates fear and resentment, creating enemies rather than allies.

Ways of speaking:

- *"This is what we're doing here, if you don't like it, tough."*
- *"This must be done this way, no matter what you think."*

Beliefs:

- *"I'm okay. You are not."*
- *"I'm superior and right, and you're inferior, and wrong."*
- *"I can dominate and intimidate you."*
- *"I can violate your rights."*
- *"You're not worth anything."*
- *"It's all your fault."*
- *"You owe me."*
- *"I own you."*

Behaviour: These individuals have difficulties expressing their emotions verbally in an open and clear manner. They usually have staring eyes, try to dominate others, and use humiliation to control others. Moreover, aggressive communicators often criticise, blame or attack others, have low frustration tolerance, and speak in a loud and demanding voice. They are not willing to listen attentively and generally use "you" statements in their interactions. Thus, they don't take responsibility for their words, deeds, and actions.

Consequences: Aggressive communicators often feel angry and resentful within as they tend to blame others for their own problems. They often generate fear, and hatred in others. Therefore, these people frequently make enemies and become alienated from others.

One of my clients, Max, a 46-year-old sales manager, illustrated this pattern clearly. He came to counselling after receiving feedback from his team that they found him "intimidating" and "hard to talk to." Max dismissed these comments at first, insisting, *"They're just too sensitive. Someone has to take charge."* He viewed his bluntness as a sign of strength and control.

At his workplace, Max often interrupted others mid-sentence, speaking over them in a loud, and firm tone. When a team member would propose a new idea, he would quickly counter with, *"That won't work - we'll do it my way,"* or *"You clearly didn't think this through."* His colleagues would fall silent, exchanging uncomfortable glances. Deep down, Max noticed that people avoided him, but he justified it by telling himself, *"They respect me too much to argue."* Beneath his confidence, however, Max often felt tense and on the edge. He admitted that when someone disagreed with him, he felt a surge of anger and a strong urge to "win the argument."

In counselling, he eventually revealed a deeper layer - a fear of being seen as weak or incompetent. *"I grew up with a father who said only the tough ones survive,"* he said. *"If I don't stay in control, I feel week and vulnerable."* Over time, Max began to recognise that his aggressive communication wasn't strength - it was armour. It protected him from vulnerability but also kept him isolated. He noticed that, despite being in a leadership role, he felt increasingly lonely and disconnected.

Under my guidance, Max learned to pause before reacting, to focus on his breath, and to shift from accusatory "you" statements to more mindful "I" statements, such as, *"I feel frustrated when deadlines aren't met, and I'd like us to find a solution together."* This subtle change helped him express his needs clearly without attacking others.

As Max practised listening attentively and communicating assertively, his team began to respond differently. Meetings became more collaborative, and he noticed that the members of his team started sharing their ideas again. Over time, Max's relationships at work improved, and he described feeling "lighter" and less defensive. What surprised him most was realising that true authority doesn't come from control or fear - but from respect and genuine connection.

Beneath aggressive behaviour often lie unacknowledged fears and vulnerabilities. But anger is not always expressed in direct or visible ways. Sometimes it takes a subtler form - concealed beneath pleasant words or quiet compliance. This brings us to another common pattern of communication - one that blends the silence of passivity with the inner tension of aggression.

Passive-Aggressive Communication Style

Passive-aggressive communication is a style in which individuals appear passive on the surface, but they are acting out anger or other negative emotions in a subtle, indirect, or behind the scenes way. People who develop this pattern of communication usually feel powerless, stuck, and resentful inside. In other words, these individuals feel incapable of dealing directly with the target of their resentment. Instead, they express their anger or frustration by subtly undermining the person they resent. They may procrastinate, give backhanded comments, or subtly sabotage others. This often leaves those around them feeling confused, hurt, or frustrated.

Ways of speaking:

- *"Fine...Whatever..."*
- *"Why don't you go ahead, and do it? My ideas aren't very good, anyway."*
- *"You always know better in any case."*
- *"I thought you knew."*

Beliefs:

- *"I'm weak and resentful. So, I sabotage, frustrate, and disrupt."*
- *"I'm powerless to deal with you head on. So, I must use the strategy to hit you and run away."*
- *"I will appear cooperative, but I'm not."*

Behaviour: These individuals usually mutter to themselves rather than confronting the person, or trying to solve the issue at hand. They have difficulty recognising and acknowledging their own negative emotions. Hence, they often use facial expressions that don't match their true feelings. For example, they may smile when they feel angry. In other words, they often deny that there is a problem. Also, they usually appear cooperative while purposely doing things to annoy and disrupt others. Passive-aggressive communicators may also use subtle sabotage to get even.

Consequences: These individuals usually discharge anger and resentment while not properly addressing the real issues. As a result, they often become alienated from those around them. Unfortunately, if they continue to use this manner of communication, they won't be able to grow and mature and will remain in a state of powerlessness.

In my counselling practice, I worked with Olivia, a 39-year-old researcher, who illustrated this pattern clearly. When her colleagues made suggestions or requests, she often responded with a seemingly indifferent tone, saying things like, *"Fine... whatever you think."* On the surface, Olivia appeared cooperative and agreeable, yet underneath, she felt frustrated and quietly wronged. She often told herself, *"They don't care about my ideas, so why bother speaking up?"*

Later, in private, Olivia would vent her irritation to her friends, complaining that her input at work was consistently overlooked or undervalued. Sometimes, she would procrastinate or "forget" to complete her tasks assigned by the colleagues she resented - small acts that expressed her unspoken anger. Though subtle, these behaviours left her colleagues confused and occasionally frustrated, sensing that something was amiss but unable to pinpoint what.

When Olivia came to counselling, she recognised a pattern: she felt powerless to assert herself openly, so she expressed her negative feelings indirectly. This passive-aggressive cycle left her feeling stuck, resentful, and isolated, even though she wished for connection and recognition. Through counselling, she began to identify the sources of her resentment and to explore her underlying fears of confrontation.

As she reflected on her past, Olivia realised that these fears did not arise in the workplace alone. They had been shaped over many years by earlier experiences, where speaking up often led to criticism, dismissal, or emotional withdrawal from the people she depended on. As a child, she had learned - often painfully - that expressing her needs or disagreeing openly could result in conflict, rejection, or being labelled "difficult." To protect herself, she developed the belief that staying quiet was safer than risking disapproval. Over time, this self-protective strategy became automatic. Even as an accomplished professional, Olivia still carried the old fear that direct communication would expose her to judgement or hostility. Confrontation, in her mind, was synonymous with danger.

Once she uncovered these deeper roots, Olivia began to understand that her passive-aggressive communication was not a character flaw, but a long-standing coping mechanism. This insight allowed her to approach herself with greater compassion and to gradually develop healthier, more confident ways of expressing her needs. Olivia practised expressing her feelings in small, direct, and calm ways, such as saying, *"I'd like to be included in planning, too,"* or *"I have an idea that might help us here."* Over time, these kinds of statements became natural, allowing her to communicate honestly, without hiding behind sarcasm or inaction.

Her colleagues soon noticed the change. Teamwork improved, discussions became more collaborative, and trust grew. For Olivia, breaking the pattern of silent compliance and subtle rebellion brought a sense of empowerment and relief - she no longer carried the weight of unspoken anger and could engage authentically and confidently with those around her.

This transformation highlights a crucial truth: the most effective style of communication - the one each of us needs to develop to communicate successfully and authentically - is assertiveness.

Assertive Communication Style

Assertiveness is the cornerstone of healthy and effective communication. Assertive communicators express their thoughts, feelings, and needs clearly and respectfully, without violating others' rights. These individuals value themselves, their time, and their needs. Importantly, they are able to meet their own needs while being highly respectful of the rights of others.

While communicating with others, they are polite but firm, being able to express their opinions, feelings, and boundaries in a calm and confident manner. Moreover, their facial expressions and actions fit with their spoken words. Therefore, this communication style fosters mutual understanding, respect, and cooperation.

Ways of speaking:

- *"That's a good idea. And how about if we did this too?"*
- *"I can see that, but I'd really like..."*
- *"I understand your point of view. Thank you for sharing it with me. What I believe we can do is...."*

Beliefs:

- *"I'm okay. You are okay."*
- *"We are equally entitled to express ourselves openly and respectfully to one another."*
- *"I speak clearly, honestly, and to the point."*
- *"I can't control others, but I can control myself."*
- *"I realise I have choices in my life, and I thoughtfully consider my options."*
- *"I place a high priority on having my rights respected, and I respect the rights of others."*
- *"I am one hundred percent responsible for my own happiness."*

Behaviour: These individuals generally behave in a warm, relaxed, and an open manner. When interacting with others, they also maintain comfortable and natural eye contact.

Consequences: Assertive communicators usually develop good relationships with others, as they are feeling at peace both with themselves and others. Consequently, they are generally happy with the outcomes of the situations in life.

Having understood what assertiveness looks like, the next step is learning how to develop it in your own life.

How to Become Assertive

Assertiveness is a skill - and like any skill, it can be learned, strengthened, and mastered with consistent practice. Even if you are not used to be assertive, you can cultivate this ability by learning how to express yourself clearly, respectfully, and confidently. Assertive communication means expressing your thoughts and feelings honestly while also respecting the rights, needs, and boundaries of others.

A key element of assertive communication is using "I" statements. These statements allow you to take responsibility for your own feelings and experiences rather than blaming others.

This approach reduces defensiveness, fosters understanding, and helps you stay grounded and calm, even in difficult conversations.

To support you in developing this skill, the following structure provides a simple, practical formula you can rely on during challenging interactions. With practice, it becomes a natural and empowering way of communicating.

A Handy Structure for Assertive Communication

1. Pause and focus on your breathing before speaking.

This helps you regulate your emotions, gather your thoughts, and stay anchored in calmness rather than reacting impulsively.

2. Request a good time to talk in private.

This shows respect for the other person and ensures you both have the space and focus needed for a meaningful conversation.

3. Begin with a sincere compliment or expression of goodwill.

This sets a positive tone, reduces tension, and signals that your intention is constructive, not confrontational.

4. State the facts of the situation calmly and respectfully, without exaggeration.

Describe what happened objectively - just the observable behaviour, not your interpretation of it. This helps prevent defensiveness.

5. Use "I" statements to express your genuine feelings.

For example: *"When you said this, I felt hurt/ frustrated/sad..."*

This is where you take ownership of your internal experience without accusing or blaming.

6. Explain your perspective.

Clarify why you felt the way you did: *"I felt this way because..."*

This helps the other person understand the impact of their actions more clearly.

7. Offer an alternative that respects both parties.

Suggest a constructive way forward: *"What I would like in the future is..." or "What I suggest is..."*

This transforms the conversation from complaint into collaborative problem-solving.

8. Invite the other person's perspective.

This final step encourages mutual understanding and reinforces respect.

You may ask:

- *"How do you see this situation?"*
- *"What do you think could help us move forward?"*
- *"Is there anything you need from me, so we can resolve this together?"*
- *"What changes do you think would work well for both of us?"*

This transforms the conversation into a true dialogue, ensuring that both people feel heard and included in creating the solution.

Example in Action

Instead of saying, *"You always ignore me in meetings!"* an assertive communicator may say:

"I really appreciate your professionalism and the support you give to the team. However, I felt hurt in the meeting when my suggestion wasn't acknowledged, as it made me feel that my input wasn't fully valued. In the future, I'd love the chance to share my ideas and hear your thoughts on them. How do you see this situation?"

Just as assertive communication can strengthen relationships at work, it can also bring more harmony at home. One useful tool for this is the *"DEAR MAN technique"*, which helps you express your needs clearly and respectfully in personal situations.

Here is the *"DEAR MAN"* technique:

- **Describe:** *"I noticed that the dishes were left in the sink overnight."*

- **Express:** *"I feel a bit stressed when that happens."*

- **Assert:** *"Could we agree to wash them before going to bed?"*

- **Reinforce:** *"That way, we'll both wake up to a clean and pleasant kitchen."*

- **Stay Mindful, Appear Confident,** and **Negotiate** if needed.

To communicate effectively, it is also important to reflect back what the other person has said. You can do this by repeating the actual words or by paraphrasing what you've heard in your own words - without changing their intended meaning. The paraphrasing or summarising supports the communication in two ways:

- It signals to the person that you have heard the points they just made.

- The brief summary helps you register what you have heard. Moreover, it gives the speaker an opportunity to clarify any misunderstandings.

In the act of communication, it can be also helpful to notice the speaker's non-verbal cues, such as when they appear confused or uneasy. When you register these unpleasant feelings, you may ask, *"Would you like me to explain that part again?"* or, *"You look uncertain, what can I do to help?"* This reduces any tension and keeps the conversation collaborative.

You may also acknowledge the other person's feelings by reflecting back with comments, such as: *"It seems that you have doubts about asking for some extra help,"* or *"You seem /sound concerned about this…"*

Sometimes, when communicating with others, you can decrease tension in problem situations with humour, decrease the tone of your voice, or offer a smile as you make your point. All of this may ease difficult conversations and create space for genuine connection.

To begin translating these ideas into action, it is helpful to explore your own communication patterns and practise assertiveness in a structured way. The following exercise is designed to guide you in identifying your default style, experimenting with assertive responses, and gradually building this communication skill into your daily interactions.

A Practical Exercise: Exploring Your Communication Style

To better understand your own communication style and begin practising assertiveness, try the following steps:

Step 1. Self-Reflection

Think about a recent situation where you communicated with someone at work, at home, or in a friendship. Ask yourself:

- *"Did I stay silent and avoid expressing my needs?" (Passive)*

- *"Did I speak in a way that overpowered or dismissed the other person?" (Aggressive)*

- *"Did I seem agreeable at first, but later express my frustration indirectly?" (Passive-aggressive)*

- *"Or did I clearly and respectfully express my opinions, feelings, and needs?" (Assertive)*

Write down your observations.

Step 2. Rewrite the Conversation

Choose one example where you were passive, aggressive, or passive-aggressive. Rewrite how you could have responded more assertively using this structure:

- *"When you [describe the situation or the unacceptable behaviour factually], I felt [express your true feelings]. I felt this way because [explain your perspective on the situation]. What I would like in the future is [offer an alternative or a solution]."*

Example:

Instead of saying, *"Fine, do whatever you want"* (passive-aggressive), you might say:

"When you decided the plan for the weekend without asking me, I felt left out because I wanted to contribute. Next time, I'd like to be included in the decision-making process."

Step 3. Role-Play Practice

If possible, practise this rewritten conversation with a trusted friends, partner, or colleague.

Take turns role-playing different communication styles: passive, aggressive, passive-aggressive, and assertive. Notice how do you feel, both as the speaker and as the listener.

Step 4. Daily Micro-Practice

Each day, commit to one small act of assertiveness. It could be as simple as:

- Saying, *"I'd prefer tea instead of coffee."*
- Expressing, *"I need a few minutes of quiet to finish this task."*
- Or politely disagreeing in a meeting: *"I see your point, but I'd like to share another perspective."*

Remember, mastering any skill takes practice and patience. Being assertive, at first, may feel unfamiliar or even uncomfortable, but with consistent effort, it will become your second nature. Learning to communicate assertively is not just about improving your relationships - it is about honouring your feelings, valuing your needs, and claiming your voice.

Each time you speak up with clarity, honesty, and respect, you strengthen your self-confidence, nurture healthier connections, and deepen your sense of self-worth. Over time, assertive communication will transform not just how others perceive you, but also how you experience yourself - empowered, respected, and fully in charge of your own life.

Influencing Others at Work Effectively

"Great leaders don't set out to be a leader... They set out to make a difference."
- Author Unknown

Q: How can we influence others in the workplace effectively?

A: Influence is an extraordinary asset in the professional world. Gaining influence within a team makes you more respected and appreciated. It also ensures that your voice and opinions are heard and acknowledged. Moreover, building influence in the workplace helps you collaborate more productively and effectively. Positive influence offers numerous benefits, yet like any other skill in life, developing it takes time and effort.

The reality is that each of us carries the "magic wand" of influence. It lies in influencing our own mindset and behaviours. True influence is about understanding ourselves and recognising the impact we have on others. As Albert Schweitzer wisely noted: *"Example is not the main thing in influencing others. It is the only thing."* Thus, to be an effective influencer, you need to become a positive role-model. Behaving in the way you wish others to behave can influence them, often without you even realising it.

Core Principles of Building Influence at Work

To increase your influence at work, you need to:

- **Cultivate reliability through consistency.**

Consistency is the foundation of influence. When your words or deeds are inconsistent or unpredictable, your colleagues may find it hard to know if they can rely on you. In fact, inconsistency is the fastest way to erode trust within your team. On the contrary, by being consistent in your words, actions, and principles, you will cultivate a reputation of authority, and establish yourself as a credible person.

- **Develop trust with your co-workers.**

Your ability to influence others expands in

direct proportion to the level of trust your co-workers feel towards you. Without trust, no title or expertise will make your colleagues listen. Altering the truth, even slightly, can quickly break that trust. Therefore, you need to cultivate trust by being open and honest at all times.

- **Identify what's common between yourself and your colleagues.**

Regardless of differences in age, gender, background, or beliefs, you can always find something you share with others - whether it is a goal, a value, or a passion - if you seek it out. Judging others leaves little room for genuine trust and collaboration. By contrast, focusing on what you share in common creates a strong foundation for connection and trust.

- **Discover areas of collaboration.**

Influence grows when you step into true collaboration. Begin by finding one area important to your colleague and offer to help. True collaboration requires to let go of your ego, as well as of any impulses you may have to make decisions entirely on your own. Remember, true influence is about partnership, not dominance.

- **Take time to get to know your co-workers.**

Influence requires understanding what makes people feel valued. Listen to their stories, learn what helps them increase their self-esteem, and share your own experiences to foster mutual respect.

- **Ask important questions and listen deeply.**

Encourage your co-workers to speak up, especially if they don't often voice their own opinions. Importantly, listen to everyone's opinion. Take time to listen in a loving and respectful manner, acknowledge their opinions, and let them know that you value them. Deep listening makes others feel respected and open to your influence.

- **Be assertive, but not aggressive.**

Assertiveness means expressing your ideas with confidence while respecting others' rights, opinions and feelings. Assertiveness commands respect without alienating others. Aggression, on the other hand, creates fear, damages trust and weakens influence.

- **Express genuine gratitude to your co-workers.**

When expressing gratitude to your co-workers, remember to show their value in an appropriate context. Be specific, concise, and truthful. It is also important to show the connection between their actions, and the benefits for the company. For example, instead of saying, *"Thanks for your help,"* you could say: *"Thank you for taking the time to revise the client report. Your attention to detail not only made the report more accurate but also helped us meet the deadline, which strengthened our client's trust in the team."* Remember, gratitude reinforces people's positive behaviours and deepens relationships.

- **Believe in your co-workers.**

The more you believe in the people around you and incorporate their ideas into your vision, the more they will believe in your ideas and integrate them into their work habits. When you show faith in others, they will often rise to meet - and even surpass - your expectations.

- **Inspire your co-workers to new levels of achievement.**

Positive encouragement can unlock hidden potential. Inspire and motivate your co-workers with uplifting words, wise guidance, and unconditional support that help them recognise the greatness within themselves.

Give them sincere compliments, notice their strengths, and let them know what you truly value in them. For example, instead of simply saying, *"Good job on the presentation,"* you could say: *"Your presentation today was excellent - I especially appreciated how clearly you explained the complex data. Your ability to make it understandable not only impressed the team but also inspired us to aim higher in our own projects."*

Genuine appreciation creates a ripple effect of positivity. People are more receptive to influence when they feel truly valued. By doing so, you will not only empower others but also become a truly influential leader.

If you apply these principles consistently in your professional life, you will become the driving force behind a more collaborative and uplifting workplace environment. You will influence others not through force or authority, but through trust, respect, and inspiration. Then, your colleagues will see you as a leader because of the value you bring, and the way you make them feel. Remember, the world needs your voice, knowledge, and vision. Act now, and soon you will reach your full potential as a powerful leader in this world.

To help you cultivate this influence more consciously, try the following practice:

Practical Exercise: Workplace Influence Journal

Take a few quiet minutes to reflect in your *"Workplace Influence Journal."* Writing your thoughts will help you identify the areas where you already create positive impact - and the spaces where your influence can expand even further.

Step 1: Self-Reflection

Ask yourself:

- *How do I currently influence others at work?*
- *Do I lead more by example - by words, or by actions?*
- *Which of the four communication styles (passive, aggressive, passive-aggressive, or assertive) do I use most often at work?*

Step 2: Identify One Strength

Write down one way you already influence others positively. For example: *"I always follow through* on deadlines, so my team knows they can rely on me."

Step 3: Spot One Growth Area

Choose one principle from this chapter that you would like to strengthen (e.g., consistency, collaboration, communication). For instance: *"I need to practise being more assertive in our meetings."*

Step 4: Choose One Action and Apply It

Select one small action that you will practise this week.

Examples:

- *I will start each meeting by acknowledging a colleague's contribution.*

- *I will write down every commitment I make and check it off when completed.*

- *I will ask one co-worker what I can do to make their work easier.*

Step 5: Review and Reflect

At the end of the week, return to your journal and write:

- *What did I try?*

- *How did my co-workers respond?*

- *How did I feel?*
- *What did I learn about my ability to influence others?*

Remember that influence is born not from grand gestures or dramatic speeches, but from the steady rhythm of daily respect, encouragement, and reliability. It is in these small, consistent actions that your true leadership will shine.

Achieving Material Abundance

---

*"The way of abundance is a one-way street.
You are either heading for lack, or heading for
abundance."*
- Florence Scovel Shinn

Q: How can we create material abundance in our lives?

A: What you focus on with your thoughts and words is what you attract in life. If your thoughts, spoken words, and corresponding feelings dwell on lack and limitation, that is exactly what you will experience. Conversely, if you are constantly thinking and talking about material abundance and professional success, that will be reflected in your reality. Remember, thoughts and feelings about riches produce rich conditions! Therefore, to attract financial abundance, first you must believe that you are already rich and successful.

One of the most powerful ways to believe and feel that you are already abundant is to cultivate sincere gratitude for what you already have. Begin by noticing and appreciating the resources, opportunities, and blessings that are already present in your life - no matter how small they may seem. Remember, each moment of thankfulness reinforces the sense that you are already rich in some way, creating fertile ground for even more abundance to flow into your life.

To put this into practice, you can focus on three key steps:

- **Acknowledge your possessions and achievements:** Reflect on your skills, your home, your income, your relationships, or your daily comforts. Recognising these is a reminder that your life already contains richness.

- **Express your gratitude:** Speak it aloud, write it down in a journal, or share it with others. Saying, *"I am grateful for this opportunity"* or *"I appreciate the support I receive from my colleagues"* strengthens the feeling of abundance within you.

- **Feel the gratitude deeply:** Don't just list your blessings - allow yourself to experience the warmth, satisfaction, and joy of appreciation. The more you truly feel it, the more your mindset will shift from scarcity to abundance.

By consistently practising gratitude for what you already have, you will align your thoughts and emotions with richness. This will create a natural magnet for material success and professional opportunities, allowing abundance to flow effortlessly into your life.

However, belief alone is not enough. To manifest abundance and success, your energy needs direction - a clear and definite purpose that will channel your thoughts and actions towards a meaningful goal. Without a definite purpose, you are like a ship without a rudder, drifting wherever the currents of life may carry you. But when you have a clear and definite purpose - one that is firmly fixed in your mind - you become like a guided projectile, moving with unstoppable determination towards your chosen destination.

A clear sense of purpose gives direction to your energy, focus to your actions, and meaning to your existence. It transforms confusion into clarity and hesitation into decisive movement. This truth is not merely theoretical - it is something I've lived and experienced in my own life. Let me share my true personal story with you which I hope will inspire and encourage you on your own path towards prosperity.

My Story

For about seven years, I worked as a general practitioner in Skopje, the capital of my native country, Macedonia. Yet deep inside, I've always felt a quiet calling - a desire to understand the human mind and help others heal emotionally and spiritually.

Several years later, when my husband and I migrated to Australia with our 18-month-old son, our lives were filled with uncertainty. We left behind our family, our friends, and our financial stability, arriving in a new country with very little money or social support. There were days when even buying basic groceries felt like a struggle. I still remember standing in the supermarket aisle, calculating what we could afford, and feeling a deep longing - not just for money, but for a sense of abundance, security, and freedom.

It was precisely during those moments of scarcity, when my life felt uncertain and fragile, that a quiet yet powerful sense of purpose began to stir within me. Rather than succumbing to fear or despair, I made a deliberate choice to shift my attention from what I lacked to the treasures already present in my life - love, health, the unwavering support of my family, and the precious opportunity to start anew. I felt a spark of hope igniting inside me, a whisper that reminded me of my deeper calling.

With this renewed focus, I consciously realigned my life with my true passion -psychology. Each step forward was fuelled not by external validation, but by the inner conviction that I could create meaning and growth from even the most challenging circumstances. Driven by this inner purpose, I completed a Diploma in Counselling and went on to earn a PhD in Psychology at Deakin University in Melbourne. Although it was not easy - balancing full-time study with caring for our two primary school children after school - I managed to complete my PhD journey both timely and successfully.

Every single day, I practised gratitude, taking time to acknowledge the blessings I already possessed, and I visualised a brighter, more fulfilling future. Even when the world around me seemed to offer no proof that my dreams were attainable, I held onto that vision with unwavering faith. That faith became my guiding light, turning fear into courage, scarcity into abundance, and uncertainty into a profound sense of possibility.

Gradually, my inner dialogue began to transform. Instead of thinking, *"I can't afford this,"* I shifted to *"I am choosing to spend my money wisely as I create more wealth."* When fear whispered, *"I have no control over my future,"* I reminded myself, *"I am the master of my fate."* And whenever doubt crept in with, *"I will never have enough,"* I affirmed, *"I am creating a life of prosperity and abundance."*

Along this journey, I also discovered the transformative power of giving. Even when I had very little, I always chose to share what I could with others - whether it was a small donation to someone in need, a gesture of gratitude to someone who helped me, or simply offering a kind word or a smile to a stranger.

By giving from my heart, my belief that *"I don't have enough"* gradually transformed into *"I have more than enough to share with others - money, a smile, or an encouraging word - and to bring them joy immediately."* This simple yet profound attitude of giving opened a new flow of positive energy in my life. The more I gave, the more I received - not only in material terms, but in love, opportunities, and blessings. Over time, my outer world started to mirror my inner transformation. Step by step, every act of courage, gratitude, and giving brought me closer to the life I had once only imagined.

Today, I am a fulfilled and financially abundant author of motivational self-help books, an internationally recognised counsellor, and motivational speaker. My book trilogy, *"Another Way of Living"*, has touched thousands of lives across the globe - helping people find their inner peace, transform their limiting beliefs, and open themselves to material abundance and success.

Most importantly, from my own journey, I learned a timeless truth: true abundance begins in the heart. It grows through gratitude, and it multiplies through giving. But it also requires something deeper - a definite purpose. Without it, your energy scatters and your effort dissolves. With it, everything you think, say, and do moves in harmony towards your vision.

The Blessing of Giving

When your purpose is clear, gratitude flows naturally, and giving becomes a heartfelt, effortless expression. Therefore, to attract material abundance and lasting success, cultivate a heart full of appreciation for all you already have, and offer freely from that place of gratitude. Remember, giving always precedes receiving - for whatever is offered with genuine love - returns blessed and multiplied. When you live with a spirit of generosity, love, and compassion, the world around you will reflect that energy back to you in the form of kindness, opportunities, and prosperity. Through this beautiful exchange of giving and receiving, abundance will become a natural part of your life.

Consider Andrew Carnegie, one of the wealthiest and most influential men of the 19th century. While he amassed extraordinary wealth by building the American steel industry, he believed that true abundance came from giving back. Carnegie didn't just see money as a personal reward - he saw it as a tool to create lasting impact. Over his lifetime, he donated most of his fortune to build libraries, schools, universities, and foundations, giving millions of people access to education, knowledge, and opportunities that would otherwise have been out of reach.

By giving so generously, Carnegie multiplied not only the reach of his wealth but also his legacy. His philanthropy inspired others to contribute, creating a ripple effect that extended far beyond his lifetime. In essence, his abundance was not measured solely by what he accumulated but by how he empowered others to grow, learn, and succeed. Carnegie's life exemplifies a powerful truth: when we give selflessly from our heart, we create a cycle in which our generosity returns to us in ways that enrich our lives and the lives of others.

The Power of Faith

The most important step in attracting material abundance is to cultivate unwavering faith that what you desire will be granted. Believe wholeheartedly that your request is already on its way, and acknowledge in advance the experience or financial condition you wish to receive. For example, you may say, *"I am grateful for the financial freedom that is already flowing into my life."* Or *"Thank you, God, for bringing me more money and success in my life."* Then, act as though your dreams have already been fulfilled. Walk, speak, and make decisions from the mindset of someone who is already abundant. By aligning your thoughts, words, and actions with this belief, you will create the conditions for your desires to manifest.

Emphasising the critical importance of one's attitude in attracting abundance, in his brilliant book *"The Science of Getting Rich"*, the author Wallace Wattles wrote:

"The riches you receive will be in exact proportion to the definiteness of your vision, the fixity of your purpose, the steadiness of your faith, and the depth of your gratitude."

Now that you understand the inner principles of material abundance - meaningful purpose, unwavering faith, sincere gratitude, and the attitude of giving - let's put them into daily practice.

Daily Abundance Routine

Believing that you are rich and successful can be difficult at first, at it can feel unrealistic, especially if you are struggling with bills, debt, or financial stress. The key is to train your mind gradually, so that this belief becomes natural rather than forced. To make this process simple and actionable, here is a step-by-step routine that you can begin practising today:

1. Start with Small Proofs of Abundance

Belief grows from evidence. Instead of trying to convince yourself that you will become a millionaire overnight, start noticing and appreciating the abundance you already have in your life:

- A warm home, a meal on the table, or even a smile from a stranger.
- Write these down daily in a *"Proof of Abundance Journal."*

Over time, your subconscious mind will begin to accept that you already live in an abundant world.

2. Use "Bridge" Affirmations

Begin your day by looking into the mirror and saying powerful money affirmations. Speak them with confidence, devotion, and emotion, as if they are already true. If saying, *"I am rich"* feels fake, use softer, more believable affirmations that bridge the gap, such as:

- *I am open to wealth flowing into my life.*
- *I am deeply grateful for the money and the material possessions I already have.*
- *Money flows easily and effortlessly in my life.*

- *Each day, I am growing richer and more successful.*
- *All the money I have brings joy to me, and to everyone whose hearts I touch.*

Repeat these affirmations until your inner state matches your words. As these beliefs grow stronger, you can shift into more powerful "I am" statements, such as *"I'm rich and successful."*

To deepen your practice, you can find more powerful money affirmations on my YouTube channel *Dr Snezhana* (which currently has more than 30 000 followers from all around the world). I especially recommend the video *"35 Money Affirmations to Attract Financial Abundance"*.

3. Use Visualisation with Emotion

The brain cannot tell the difference between a vividly imagined experience and a real one. By visualising yourself as already rich and successful - feeling the joy of financial freedom, seeing yourself in your dream home, or experiencing your desired lifestyle -you begin to reprogram your subconscious mind to accept this as your reality.

Jim Carrey's story is a powerful example: Before becoming a world-famous actor, he wrote himself a check for $10 million for *"acting services rendered"* and dated it five years into the future. He carried it in his wallet, visualised abundance daily, and expressed gratitude as if it had already come true. Within that time, he signed a movie deal worth exactly $10 million.

4. Anchor the Feeling of Wealth in Your Daily Life

Make decisions with the confidence of someone who is already abundant. Ask yourself: *"How would the successful, wealthy version of me act in this situation?"* Then, act accordingly:

- Treat yourself to fresh flowers, a nice cup of coffee, or dressing as though you are already rich and successful.

- Walk with confidence, carry yourself with dignity, and make decisions from abundance, not fear.

These small actions will train your body, mind and soul to feel wealthy before material wealth arrives in your life.

5. Practise Generosity

Decide one act of giving for the day. It could be donating money, helping a colleague, or simply giving someone your time, undivided attention, and encouragement. But whatever you give, give it wholeheartedly, with a blessing. Remember that giving precedes receiving!

6. Surround Yourself with Abundance Energy

- Read inspiring success stories and biographies of successful people.

- Connect with people who are prosperous.

- Listen to positive money affirmations or guided abundance meditations.

This repeated exposure gradually will shift your limiting beliefs into empowering ones. When you replace your negative thoughts of fear, lack, and scarcity with personal positive affirmations of what you truly desire, you will see positive changes being manifested in your life.

Remember: you were born to thrive, not merely to survive. You are destined for a life filled with purpose, prosperity, and abundance.

Forming and Maintaining Positive Relationships

"The beginning of love is to let those we love be perfectly themselves, and not to twist them to fit our own image. Otherwise, we love only the reflection of ourselves we find in them."
- Thomas Merton

Q: Many human relationships are falling apart easily in today's modern age. How can we form and maintain positive relationships with others?

A: Lack of love and the presence of fear within is the main cause of why human relationships fail. In essence, fear is the underlying reason behind people's tendency to judge others, to withhold trust, and even to perceive others as potential threats. It is important to understand that a judgemental attitude will always misinterpret the words and actions of others, inevitably leading to separation and disconnection.

I once worked with a woman named Crystal, whose story beautifully illustrates how fear can quietly erode love. At 42, she came to counselling feeling lost and disconnected in her marriage. She often told me with tears in her eyes, *"No matter what Alexander says, I always feel like he's pointing out my flaws."*

Deep down, she longed to feel loved and accepted, yet almost everything her husband said seemed to confirm her fear of not being good enough. When Alexander would make a simple comment like, *"The dinner is a bit salty tonight,"* Crystal's heart would tighten - she immediately heard, *"You've failed again."* Even casual remarks such as, *"Maybe we should leave earlier next time,"* felt like subtle accusations that she was careless or disorganised.

What she didn't realise was that her husband's words were not the source of her pain - her own inner critic was. Crystal had spent years striving to be "perfect", silently judging herself for every perceived mistake. This constant self-criticism became a filter through which she heard everything her husband said. So, even his most neutral or affectionate words were distorted by her inner fear and self-doubt.

Through counselling, Crystal slowly began to notice this inner pattern. She started catching herself in those reactive moments, and gently asked herself, *"Is this really what he said - or is this my fear speaking?"* *"Is this really criticism, or am I projecting my own insecurities?"* At first, it wasn't easy. But as she practised this awareness, something began to soften inside her. She realised that Alexander wasn't her enemy - her own fear was.

As this understanding deepened, Crystal's perception of her husband began to change. Instead of assuming the worst, she paused, took a breath, and listened with new ears. She stopped jumping to conclusions and started giving him the benefit of the doubt. When he made a suggestion, she began to hear it as support rather than judgement. When he pointed something out, she could recognise his intention to help, not criticise. And when he expressed an opinion, she no longer interpreted it as a threat to her worth but simply as his perspective.

This shift gradually transformed her attitude towards him. She became less defensive, more open, and more receptive. She allowed herself to trust his love, instead of bracing for imagined criticism. She responded from a calmer, steadier place - a place rooted in self-compassion rather than fear. And for the first time in years, when he spoke, she could finally hear the warmth, care, and affection behind his words.

As Crystal's perception shifted from fear to trust, their relationship transformed. The arguments lessened, and laughter slowly returned to their home. She began to feel emotionally safe again - not because her husband changed, but because she changed the way she related to herself, and the way she listened.

This example beautifully illustrates a deeper truth: a judgemental attitude, born from fear, always distorts how we perceive others. When we listen through fear, we hear only judgement, blame and separation. But when we listen through love - understanding and connection naturally arise.

The reality is that each of us sees the world through the lens of our own subjective perceptions. Hence, whatever you think or say about others reveals more about you than about them. As Dr Wayne Dyer wisely noted, *"When you judge another, you do not define them, you define yourself."*

Why We Judge Others

Most judgements of others stem from one of the following reasons:

- **You wouldn't allow yourself to behave that way because it would make you uncomfortable or embarrassed.**

In this case, your judgement reflects your own inner standards or moral boundaries. When you see someone behaving in a way you would find unacceptable for yourself, it can trigger discomfort or even disapproval - not because of them, but because it challenges your personal values.

- **You might display the same behaviour and, unconsciously, project it onto others.**

Often, what irritates us in others mirrors something within ourselves that we have not yet fully accepted or resolved. This psychological mechanism, known as projection, allows us to disown aspects of our own personality that we don't like by seeing them in someone else.

- **You feel jealous and find faults with those who have what you desire.**

At times, judgement arises from jealousy - a subtle form of longing disguised as criticism. When others embody qualities or possess things we secretly wish for, we may protect our self-esteem by devaluing them instead of acknowledging our desire or insecurity.

Remember, judging others will always stir unpleasant feelings within you. And more often than not, your judgemental reactions reveal your own self-judgements and your hidden insecurities. Hence, an honest look inward will show you that the feelings you project outward towards others may offer you more insight into yourself than into them. As Pema Chodron beautifully expressed, *"If we learn to open our hearts, anyone, including the people who drive us crazy, can be our teachers."*

Love as the Foundation of Every Relationship

A person who is constantly judging or comparing with others, cannot form close, trusting, and positive bonds. Therefore, when you experience any uncomfortable feelings in your relationships with others, instead of judging them, pause and ask yourself: *"What would love do now?"* Acting from love rather than reacting from fear or judgement, creates connection instead of separation.

Remember that what you do for others, you do it for yourself. This is because we are all one. We are all made from the same substance, and that is pure love. Therefore, love must be the foundation of every human relationship! Hence, in your relationships, you need to treat others as you want to be treated, and that is with unconditional love, and utmost respect at all times.

The Importance of Healthy Boundaries

Genuine love and respect also require healthy boundaries. In other words, treating others with kindness and respect does not mean tolerating abuse, disrespect, or manipulation. In such moments, the most loving act you can offer - both to yourself and to another - is to say "no" to what diminishes your peace or integrity.

Nick (51, construction manager) came to this realisation after years of quietly enduring the hurtful behaviour of a close friend who often disguised cruelty as humour. On the surface, their friendship seemed loyal and long-standing, but beneath it lay a pattern of subtle manipulation and control. His friend often undermined him with cutting remarks like, *"Face it, Nick - without me, you'd be a nobody. You should be grateful I even bother."* Or *"Honestly, how do you even manage to keep your job with how slow you are?"*

In public, his friend would make jokes at his expense - *"Here comes Nick, the expert in overcomplicating everything!"* - and laugh as others joined in. When Nick achieved something at work or shared a personal success, his friend's praise came laced with poison: *"Don't let it go to your head - it's not like you're the only one who works hard."*

Even in private conversations, the put-downs continued in more insidious ways. His friend would sigh and say things like, *"Nick, you look like an idiot when you get emotional. It's embarrassing,"* or *"You should listen to me more - I always know better than you what's best for you."* These words left him confused, guilty, and small, as though his worth constantly depended on earning his friend's approval.

Each time, Nick smiled weakly and brushed it off, telling himself, *"He's just joking - I shouldn't take it so seriously,"* or *"Maybe I'm too sensitive."* Yet deep down, he felt the sting of humiliation and the growing weight of emotional exhaustion. Each encounter left him feeling more drained and unseen, as if a quiet voice within him was whispering, *"You deserve better than this."* Over time, Nick realised that this friendship was not built on respect and care, but on power and control. The more he tolerated his friend's behaviour, the more invisible he became - not just to his friend, but to himself.

Through counselling, Nick began to see the pattern clearly for the first time. He realised that his silence had not kept the peace - it had only allowed the disrespect to grow. Each time he excused the hurtful comments of his friend, he was unconsciously telling himself that his own feelings didn't matter. Beneath his politeness lived a quiet fear - the fear of losing the friendship, of being seen as "too sensitive," or of standing alone.

One day in our counselling session, he said softly, *"I think I've been mistaking loyalty for love."* That insight became a turning point. Together, we explored how his friend's behaviour reflected not his worth, but his friend's need to control and dominate. For the first time, Nick began to understand that respect is not earned by enduring pain - it is upheld by honouring yourself. With practice, he learned to speak from a calm and grounded place. The next time his friend mocked him, he met his eyes and said, *"When you speak to me that way, I feel disrespected. I value our friendship, but I won't tolerate being belittled."* His voice trembled slightly, but his message was clear.

At first, his friend laughed dismissively, saying, *"Oh, come on, can't you take a joke?"* But Nick didn't engage. He repeated quietly, *"I'm serious. This isn't funny to me anymore."* That moment marked the beginning of change - not in his friend, but in himself.

When the disrespect continued, Nick made the difficult decision to step back from the relationship. He felt sadness, but also relief - a deep exhale of freedom he hadn't known he was holding. In place of constant tension, there was peace. In place of self-doubt, there was quiet strength. In time, he realised that walking away was not an act of rejection, but an act of deep self-respect and genuine self-love.

In the silence that followed, something beautiful happened. Instead of feeling lonely, Nick felt lighter - freer. He realised he had not lost anything of real value; rather, he had reclaimed his dignity and peace. His act of self-respect became an act of love - for himself and for life itself. As Robert Tew wisely reminds us, *"Respect yourself enough to walk away from anything that no longer serves you, grows you, or makes you happy."*

By cultivating a loving and respectful attitude - both towards yourself and others - while setting healthy boundaries, you become someone whose very presence radiates peace, love, and authenticity. You become an example of joyfulness that is inspiring, uplifting, and exhilarating. Then you can make a connection with another human being on a more fundamental level, a connection that is beyond human understanding. And this kind of relationship will nourish the deepest yearnings of your soul.

By opening your heart to love and practising respect in every interaction, you begin to experience relationships as sacred mirrors of your own growth. Yet embodying love instead of judgement takes awareness and practice. The following exercise will help you gently shift from reacting with fear, judgement or criticism to responding with love, understanding, and compassion.

Practical Exercise: Shifting from Judgement to Love

1. Daily Reflection

At the end of each day, write down one situation where you felt irritation, criticism, or judgement towards another person.

2. Look Within

Ask yourself: "*What does this reaction reveal about me?*" Is it highlighting a fear, insecurity, or unmet need within myself?

3. Shift Your Perspective

Now ask: "*What would love do in this situation?*" Imagine responding to the person from a place of compassion and understanding rather than judgement or fear.

4. Practise in Real Time

Next time a similar situation arises, pause before reacting. Take a breath, and silently repeat *"I choose love, not fear."* Then, respond with kindness, compassion, and honesty.

5. Notice the Change

Over a week, observe how your relationships shift when you bring more awareness, compassion, and love into your interactions.

Remember, the relationships you nurture with kindness, honesty, and love are not just ties between people - they are sacred bridges to the deepest truth of who you are. And when you walk across these bridges with an open heart and dignity, you enter a realm of life where joy, harmony, and profound belonging become your natural way of being.

Choosing Friends Wisely

"Choosing friends is choosing a way of life."
- Confucius

Q: How can we choose our friends wisely?

A: Your friends reveal the kind of person you are, particularly what your true values and priorities are. In essence, your friends are a mirror of yourself. Therefore, it is crucially important to choose your friends wisely.

When choosing friends, it is important to pay attention not only to what they say, but also to what they do - and especially whether their actions match their words. Words are easy to utter; they flow like wind and can charm the ear. But actions reveal the truth of one's character. What a person does when no one is watching speaks louder than what they claim to believe.

Friendship built on mere speech is fragile, for words can disguise intention. But friendship grounded in integrity - where deeds and words become one - is enduring and real. Thus, observe not only how a person treats you, but how they treat others, especially those from whom they have nothing to gain. In such quiet moments of authenticity, the soul of a true friend becomes visible. It is through these subtle observations that we come to recognise the difference between genuine and false companionship. Remember, not everyone who smiles at you walks beside you in truth.

Friends can be divided into true friends and false friends. True friends can be uplifting, supportive, and life-giving, whereas false friends can be toxic, draining, and even harmful. There is one Swedish proverb that warns: *"False friends are worse than bitter enemies,"* meaning it is more painful to be betrayed by someone you once trusted than to be hurt by someone you already knew was against you. False friends will stay with you during the good times, but once things get hard, they will leave you behind. As Christian Nestell Bovee noted, *"False friends are like our shadow, keeping close to us while we walk in the sunshine, but leaving us the instant we cross into the shade."* This is why choosing your friends mindfully is essential.

False Friends

False friends can leave deep scars on your heart and big dents on your self-confidence. They can bring you a lot of trouble and may even lead you down the wrong road in life. Such individuals cannot offer the trust, loyalty, or safety that true friendship requires - and part of your growth is learning to decide whether they have a place in your life at all.

There are three common types of false friends:

1. Flatterers

Flatterers use kind words as a tool to get your favours. They appear supportive when you have money, success, or influence, but as soon as you lose these external possessions, they will disappear from your life. Remember, you cannot trust these people because their flatter is not genuine, and they won't stand with you when you go through difficult times in life.

I remember Marina, a 47-year-old business consultant, who shared how one of her friends constantly complimented her new clothes, her big house, and her career success. At first, she felt validated and special, almost as if someone truly saw and admired her. Her friend's compliments lifted her spirits, and she looked forward to their interactions.

But over time, Marina began to notice an uncomfortable pattern. Every compliment seemed to precede a request. Sometimes it was a small favour, other times a significant ask - introductions, recommendations, even financial help. Initially, she brushed it off, telling herself that she was imagining things, or that helping friends was just part of being generous. Yet a small voice inside her began to whisper: *"Is this how a true friend should behave? Would this person still be here with me if I had nothing to offer to her?"*

These questions became a turning point. Marina started to reflect on how she felt after each encounter. Instead of warmth and mutual appreciation, she often felt emotionally drained, used, or subtly manipulated. She realised that her friend's flattery wasn't genuine affection - it was her tool to gain something in return.

When a financial setback left Marina unable to provide further help, the friend vanished overnight. At first, Marina felt stunned, as if a rug had been pulled from under her. She was confused and hurt: *"Was our connection ever real? Had I been blind to the truth all along?"* Anger followed - at her friend for betraying her trust, at herself for not seeing the truth, and at the world for seeming so unjust. But slowly, her pain transformed into clarity. Marina realised that genuine friendship isn't built on praise or convenience - it is revealed in tough times.

Reflecting on this experience, she felt a bittersweet combination of sorrow and empowerment. Marina mourned the loss of what she thought was true friendship, yet she also felt grateful for the lesson she learned. Now, she listens not just to the words people say but also observes their actions. True friends, she learned, are the ones whose loyalty holds when life gets hard, not only when life is easy.

Marina's experience is a reminder that not everyone who smiles at you has your best interests at heart. Some people hide their motives behind flattery and praise, while others conceal them behind a mask of friendliness.

2. Two-faced friends

Two-faced people pretend to be your friends, yet speak negatively about you behind your back. Those people are not sincere, as they say different things to different people about you to please others, and to get their approval. When people are two faced, the only thing you will know for sure is that you can't trust either of their faces.

One of my clients, Xavier, a 32-year-old event coordinator, came to counselling feeling devastated and betrayed. He had always considered his colleague, Oscar a close friend - someone who laughed at his jokes, and shared casual coffee breaks. He thought he could trust him, and that their friendship was genuine.

Then came the shocking discovery. While smiling and joking with Xavier, behind his back, Oscar had been spreading rumours about his competence at work. He would make small, seemingly harmless remarks to others: *"Xavier means well, but he's not exactly detail-oriented,"* or *"He's got good ideas, but they usually need a lot of polishing."* Oscar often delivered them with a laugh, as if it were friendly banter. But over time, these comments planted seeds of doubt in the team. Colleagues began questioning Xavier's reliability, overlooking his genuine contributions.

Oscar's behaviour followed a familiar pattern of hidden rivalry. In meetings, he would interrupt Xavier mid-sentence with *"Just to clarify what*

Xavier meant..." and then rephrase the idea as his own. When a problem arose, he would casually hint that Xavier had overlooked something: *"I think Xavier missed that in his report - I had to fix it last minute."* Sometimes, he would praise Xavier faintly, with a tone that belied the compliment: *"He's creative, though sometimes a bit too idealistic for the practical side of things."* Oscar also took credit for some of Xavier's ideas during staff meetings, presenting them as if they had emerged from joint discussions, subtly erasing Xavier's input. When Xavier received praise from their manager, Oscar would remark, *"He's lucky he had my help with that,"* said with a grin that disguised envy as humour.

The revelation came unexpectedly. One afternoon, during a team lunch, Xavier overheard two colleagues repeating one of Oscar's "jokes" about him - a line he had never heard before but that carried Oscar's familiar tone. Their awkward silence when they noticed him, confirmed what words could not. Later, another co-worker, moved by guilt, confided that Oscar often made such comments when Xavier wasn't around. Suddenly, scattered moments - the strange glances in meetings, the subtle change in tone from teammates, the distant smiles - all fell into place.

The realisation hit Xavier like a punch to the chest. He felt disbelief first, *"How could someone I trusted so much do this to me?"*, followed by a deep sting of hurt, as if the ground beneath him had collapsed. The betrayal felt more painful than if a stranger had done it, because this was someone he had opened up to, confided in, and valued deeply.

Xavier's mind spun with questions and self-doubt: *"Did I ever truly know him? How many others feel this way because of his words, intentions and actions?"* Anger and sadness intertwined, leaving him with a sharp sense of vulnerability. He began to understand that two-faced people are not only dishonest with you but also with themselves - they cannot sustain authenticity and prefer the illusion of others' approval over truth.

Over time, Xavier processed the experience and reflected on what it taught him. He realised that integrity and sincerity are non-negotiable qualities in a true friendship. He also understood an important truth: the way someone talks about others in front of you is often a mirror of how they speak about you when you are absent. This insight helped him rebuild trust in relationships more cautiously, choosing friends who showed loyalty, consistency, and honesty - both in private and in public.

Xavier's story illustrates how words can be used to deceive. Yet deception doesn't always come through betrayal - it can also appear in the form of empty, self-centred speech.

3. Those who talk excessively

People who talk too much, usually say too little. These kinds of friends are generally poor listeners, and they don't seem to understand that listening is an important skill to connect to others. They tend to talk predominantly about themselves trying to impress you, but they don't seem genuinely interested in you.

In general, these individuals talk a lot in order to artificially inflate others' opinions about themselves, and to cover up their low self-esteem. As a consequence, they undermine their integrity, reputation and influence, and cause feelings of frustration, and resentment in others. Their failure to make commitments can have a profound negative impact on your friendship with them, leaving you feeling drained and disappointed.

My cousin, Isabella (39) shared with me her growing frustration with a friendship that had become emotionally draining. At first, Isabella was happy to spend time with someone she considered close, thinking those meetings would be mutual exchanges. But over time, she noticed a pattern: the calls were dominated entirely by her friend, who talked endlessly about her career challenges and personal problems, rarely pausing to ask Isabella how she was doing.

Isabella felt invisible, a spectator in what should have been a shared space. *"I felt like my role was just to be her audience,"* she admitted. At first, she tried to stay patient, telling herself that she was being supportive, but slowly, a feeling of exhaustion settled in. She began to dread the calls, noticing how her energy drained instead of being replenished. Frustration and resentment quietly built up inside her: *"Why am I giving so much attention and getting so little in return? Does she even care about me?"*

Eventually, Isabella recognised that this one-sided dynamic was not just emotionally tiring - it was unsustainable. She realised that people who talk too much often fail to keep their promises, or to show genuine integrity. By stepping back, Isabella reclaimed her energy and began prioritising relationships that were reciprocal, nourishing, and rooted in mutual respect and care. This experience taught her an important lesson - listening, attention, and thoughtful actions are the true measures of friendship, not the volume of words.

Through encounters with flatterers, deceivers, and self-absorbed talkers, we learn what friendship is not. But such lessons also awaken a deeper question: *"What does it mean to be a true friend - and to have one?"*

True Friends

True friends are always honest, supportive, and faithful to you. They will always stand with you both in good and bad times. When you go through troubled times, real friends will encourage you, help you, and strengthen you to overcome your challenges quickly and easily. You can always trust them without any doubts, as deep in your heart you know that they always have good intentions for you. True friends accept you totally, allowing you to be yourself. These types of friends will support you in all your endeavours, and help you move closer to your dreams.

True friends also celebrate your successes without envy, rejoicing genuinely in your happiness. For example, one of my clients, Peter, a 39-year-old graphic designer, shared with me how his best friend threw him a small surprise party when he landed a new job. *"He was genuinely happy for me,"* Peter laughed. *"That's when I knew he wasn't just a friend - he was family."*

Observing friendships in this way can be a powerful guide for your own life. Remember that not every relationship offers the same depth of care and loyalty. Therefore, it is worth pausing to reflect on the people you choose to surround yourself with.

The quality of your friendships directly shapes the quality of your life, your sense of safety, and your emotional wellbeing. With this in mind, let's explore some questions and insights to help you choose your friends wisely.

Reflection: Choosing Friends Wisely

Take a moment to reflect on the friendships in your life. Ask yourself:

- *Can I truly trust this person?*
- *Can I turn to them when I need help?*

- *How do I feel in their presence - energised and safe, or drained and tense?*

Honest answers to these questions will guide you towards the right friendships. Also, listen to how your friends talk about others. In general, the way someone talks about others in front of you - mirrors how they speak about you when you're not around.

Ultimately, the friendships you attract reflect your inner wisdom and self-cultivation. If you want to have good friends, first cultivate a kind and loving heart yourself. Moreover, be willing to share what is in your heart and mind with those you trust. Friendships rooted in shared values are mutually respectful, satisfying, and supportive.

Most importantly, true friends will enhance your self-esteem while allowing you the freedom to remain authentic. Therefore, choose friends who radiate joy, live with purpose, and bring happiness not only to you, but also to those around them. Their loyalty, empathy, and authenticity are rare gifts that nourish the heart and soul. By choosing your friends wisely, you are shaping the quality of your inner world and the direction of your life.

Remember that even one loyal friend who loves you for who you are can illuminate your path far more than a hundred shallow connections ever could.

True Romantic Love

"Lovers don't finally meet somewhere. They're in each other all along."
- Rumi

Q: What is true romantic love? And how do you know when you have found it?

A: Without love, we cannot find everlasting happiness, because deep in ourselves, all we truly want - is to love, and to be loved for who we truly are.

True love is total and unconditional acceptance of another human being. It is selfless, offering care and affection freely, without expecting anything in return. True love does not demand, nor does it pose any conditions. Its joy lies in the pure act of sharing and giving wholeheartedly. True love brings both joy and freedom - to you and to the one you love. Remember, true unconditional love always allows free will to exist.

Sadly, very few people in our modern age have experienced true romantic love. To understand why, we need to explore the following question: *"Where did we learn about love?"* Love is first learned at home - in the way we were treated by those closest to us. Often, the significant people in our early years taught us, directly or indirectly, that to get their love and approval, we had to meet their expectations. This is how many of us came to believe that love is conditional.

As we grew, most of us carried this belief into adulthood, allowing it to shape the way we gave and received love in our romantic relationships. This is the reason why many people struggle to experience true romantic love. Those who perceive love as something to be earned rather than something to be shared, struggle to experience genuine connection with their romantic partners. Sadly, by constantly keeping their hearts closed to love, out of fear, they create their own loveless existence they wish to escape.

But there is another way - a higher vision of love that transcends fear and scarcity. The purpose of a truly loving relationship is not to fill a void, but to share your completeness with the one you choose to love - to grow, to heal, and to create the grandest version of yourselves together. Love, at its highest form, is a sacred opportunity for mutual transformation. Within such a relationship, you come to see yourself as you truly are, and awaken your highest potential in life.

The longing for love and sexual expression is one of the most powerful forces within human nature. When this energy is consciously directed and refined, it becomes a source of immense creativity, inspiration, and even genius. Yet few truly understand the profound nature of sex and its sacred connection to love. Too often, it has been misrepresented, distorted, or hidden behind shame and ignorance. In truth, the sexual impulse is not merely physical - it is a vital expression of life itself, a creative current that can elevate the human spirit when united with love and romance.

Love, sex, and romance together form the powerful triad of human emotion. Love brings balance and grace; sex provides vitality and drive; romance adds beauty and poetry to existence. When these three flow together in harmony, they awaken the highest creative and spiritual potential within a person. Without love, sexual desire may descend into jealousy, obsession, or destructiveness. But when the heart's tenderness tempers passion, it reveals the artistry and beauty inherent in every human soul. True love leaves an indelible mark upon one's Being - it refines the emotions, deepens empathy, and awakens the Divine spark within.

In marriage, happiness endures only when love and sexual intimacy are balanced and complemented by romance. Where love, romance, and the conscious understanding of sexual energy thrive, there can be no discord. Every act - however simple - becomes an expression of devotion. A true partnership founded on this triad not only nurtures the heart but also awakens the genius within, reminding us that love, in its purest and most complete form, is the highest creative power known to humankind.

When two souls meet with this awareness, love becomes more than companionship - it becomes a shared journey of awakening. To find your soulmate and share your life with that person is one of the most beautiful gifts in existence. The reality is that each of us has their "other half" - the one who mirrors our inner world and soul. As Florence Scovel Shinn wrote so beautifully, *"These are the two whom God has joined together, and no man shall (or can) part asunder."*

When you meet your soulmate - the other half of your soul - deep in your heart, you will know that instantly. You will feel a profound, unspoken connection that transcends words and time. And your love will become a wellspring of joy and bliss, flowing through every shared moment. Together, you will experience days filled with laughter, wonder, and tenderness, and nights wrapped in warmth, closeness, and peace - creating a bond that feels eternal.

Yet while the intensity of soul connection gives love its depth and magic, it is the companionship and shared understanding - the meeting of both minds and hearts - that give it endurance. Friedrich Nietzsche, one of the most influential modern thinkers, beautifully captured the essence of enduring love:

"Marriage is a long conversation. When marrying you should ask yourself this question: do you believe you are going to enjoy talking with this woman into your old age? Everything else in a marriage is transitory, but most of the time that you're together will be devoted to conversation."

These words deeply resonate with me. I have been blessed to experience this truth personally in my own life. For more than 20 years, I have enjoyed a truly fulfilling marriage with my soulmate - my husband, Emil. Our relationship is built on mutual love, respect, and understanding. We have walked through life together not by trying to change one another, but by celebrating each other's individuality while holding space for one another's growth. When challenges arise, instead of creating distance, they become opportunities for us to deepen our trust and strengthen our bond. It is this foundation of unconditional acceptance and genuine care that allows our love to keep expanding - and I know from my heart that this is possible for anyone who chooses to love this way.

If you would like to explore more about how to form and maintain a truly fulfilling relationship with your partner, I share useful practical tools, psychological research, and timeless wisdom in my book "*Love Unlocked: Decoding the Secrets of True Romantic Love.*" Here is one genuine review from a reader in the United States which beautifully reflects the essence of this book:

"*Whether you're newly married, navigating conflict, recovering from a toxic relationship, or still searching for the right one for you, this book gives you practical tools and heartfelt guidance to create the love life you deserve. Inside, you'll find:*

- *A clinically proven Compatibility Test to help couples examine their relationship with accuracy and discover how to strengthen it.*

- *A Compatibility List designed for singles and those seeking love - showing you how to attract the right partner for a fulfilling future together.*

- *Actionable strategies for stronger communication and mutual respect.*

- *Expert advice, personal stories, and proven counselling techniques to resolve conflict, deepen intimacy, and foster mutual respect."*

- Tabitha Jones, United States

Reading Tabitha's words reminds us that the practices, insights, and strategies in this book are more than techniques - they are invitations to a deeper understanding of love itself. True romantic love is unlike any other bond because it carries the paradox of self-loss and self-discovery. When you love deeply, the boundaries of "me" and "mine" dissolve into "us," and something greater than either individual emerges - a shared consciousness that expands both hearts. Love invites you to surrender and open your heart, bringing vulnerability and courage - the very qualities needed for transformation.

Yet love is not only an awakening - it is also a crucible of challenge and growth. Love acts as a mirror, reflecting your light and your shadow - your wounds, your needs, and your capacity to give and receive. It tests the ego, and brings differences and misunderstandings to the surface. Alone, the ego deceives. In the eyes of love, the truth becomes unavoidable. The friction, tension, and conflict that arise are not obstacles to love but invitations to deepen it. To love is to say, *"I trust you enough to let you see my soul,"* preparing yourself for the deeper trust of surrendering to life itself.

True love also honours the delicate balance between individuality and unity. While "me" and "mine" dissolve into "us," each person must retain their essence. A healthy, enduring love celebrates both the shared space of connection and the wholeness of each individual. It teaches that the highest intimacy does not erase the self but allows the self to flourish alongside another, creating a richer, more expansive "we."

At its highest, true romantic love becomes a rehearsal for Divine Union. In moments of deep intimacy - when time dissolves and two souls merge in trust - we glimpse the pure self that exists beyond fear, conditioning, or separation. These sacred moments remind us that we are whole, radiant, and already one with life.

To walk the path of love is to return again and again to our essence, to the home we never truly left - our original, Divine Self. For in the end, true love is not something we find - it is something we become.

You and Me

Two raindrops from the evening shower,
Two shiny headlights from the traffic ahead,
Two random notes played on the jazz radio,
Two clear imprints on the already beaten road.
One next to each other,
My soul and yours together,
Desire seeking rest,
Emptiness demanding marrow.
You and me together,
Heart to heart,
Soul to soul,
As two, but one.

Cultivating Unconditional Self-Love and Self-Acceptance

"Loving ourselves works miracles in our lives."

- Louise Hay

Q: How can I learn to love and accept myself unconditionally?

A: Self-love is the most important love of all. The way you love and treat yourself determines the way you treat others - as well as the way you think, speak and act. It affects everything in your life - your choices, your behaviours, and the quality of your relationships. Therefore, it is essential to accept yourself completely, and to become gentler, kinder, and more loving towards yourself. If you don't love and accept yourself unconditionally, someone else's love will never be enough. Moreover, unless you love yourself completely, you won't be able to love others fully.

In truth, you can love others only to the extent to which you love and accept yourself. You can offer love only to the extent that you embody it within. When you begin to love and accept yourself as you are, that love will naturally overflow and it will be reflected in all your thoughts, words, and actions.

The Cost of Non-Acceptance

Non-acceptance of yourself, others, and life itself, creates inner tension - a quiet but persistent restlessness that keeps you from feeling whole. This inner tension, in essence, is a result of your inner conflict. And this inner conflict is created and maintained by your ego, composed of all beliefs, expectations, and judgements imposed by others about how you should think, speak, and act in the society.

Through the lens of your unexamined beliefs, you perceive yourself and the world around you, and then you act on those beliefs. For example, if you carry a deep-seated belief that you are unlovable, you may unconsciously tolerate treatment that confirms that belief - staying in relationships that diminish you, avoiding opportunities where your light might shine, or dismissing genuine affection because it feels undeserved. Likewise, you may view and treat others through the same lens. In this way, your beliefs become self-fulfilling prophecies, quietly scripting the story of your life.

I have seen this truth unfold in the lives of many clients. For example, one of my clients, Lauren, a 34-year-old pharmacist, came to me convinced that she was not "good enough" to be loved. On the surface, she appeared confident, warm, and capable - yet beneath that calm exterior lived a quiet ache of loneliness and a constant fear of rejection. When someone complimented her, she would smile politely but think to herself, *"They don't really mean it. They're just being kind."*

When her partner expressed affection, a voice in her mind would whisper, *"Don't get used to this - it won't last."* Each time love approached, she instinctively braced for loss.

In her mind, Lauren often replayed old scenes from her childhood - moments when she had tried to earn love by excelling, pleasing, or staying small to avoid her parents' disapproval. She had learned to measure her worth through her "flawless" performance and others' reactions. No matter how much she achieved, it never felt enough.

Her romantic relationships mirrored her inner world. Lauren was drawn to partners who were emotionally distant or overly critical, as though each relationship subconsciously reaffirmed her belief: *"See? You're not worthy of love."* After each heartbreak, she would sit alone, consumed by self-doubt, asking herself, *"What's wrong with me? Why can't I just be enough for someone to stay?"*

In our counselling sessions, Lauren began to see that these painful patterns were not coincidences but reflections - mirrors of her own self-judgement. The love and acceptance she so desperately sought from others were the very qualities she had long withheld from herself.

At first, learning to love herself felt awkward, even unconvincing. Standing before a mirror and saying, *"I am worthy of love and respect just as I am,"* brought tears to her eyes - not because she fully believed it, but because some small part of her longed to. Yet with persistence and devotion, she began to change her inner dialogue. When her inner critic whispered, *"You'll never be enough,"* she learned to respond gently: *"I am enough. I am growing. I am changing."* When she would made mistakes, instead of punishing herself, she would ask, *"What can I learn from this?"* Lauren also began setting healthy boundaries - saying "no" when something didn't align with her values, and recognising her good qualities without guilt or self-doubt.

Gradually, something profound began to shift. The inner tension that once felt like a tight knot in her chest began to loosen. The harsh inner voice within herself softened into one of self-compassion. Lauren began to feel a quiet peace she had never known before - not because life had become easier, but because she was no longer fighting herself.

As her relationship with herself healed, her outer world began to mirror that transformation. Instead of chasing love to feel complete, she started radiating completeness from within - and that shift changed everything. When she finally met Mateo, their connection felt effortless and real. He loved her for who she truly was. With him, she felt safe to express herself fully - her laughter, her dreams, even her moments of vulnerability. He respected her opinions, valued her independence, and celebrated her growth.

Their relationship became a space of mutual acceptance and trust - a partnership built on honesty, compassion, and shared purpose. Lauren often said that meeting Mateo was like "coming home" - not because he filled an emptiness - but because he reflected back the love and wholeness she had already found within herself. Together, they discovered that true love doesn't complete you - it expands you.

Sidney Harris once wrote, *"It's surprising how many persons go through life without ever recognising that their feelings towards other people are largely determined by their feelings towards themselves. If you are not comfortable within yourself, you can't be comfortable with others."* Lauren's journey is a living testament to this truth. Once she learned to embrace herself fully - with all her virtues and flaws - love stopped being something she chased and became something she naturally radiated.

Her transformation also highlights a deeper reality: much of what we believe about ourselves is not inherently ours, but borrowed from the opinions of others. Thus, an important step in the process of self-love is releasing the hold of others' opinions about you. By consciously choosing not to let others define your worth, you can learn to love and value yourself for who you really are. As Thich Nhat Hanh wisely said, *"To be beautiful means to be yourself. You don't need to be accepted by others. You need to accept yourself."*

The Practice of Self-Love

Loving yourself unconditionally is the most courageous act you can undertake in life. Self-love begins with self-acceptance. You can start loving yourself when you stop any self-criticism or self-judgement. Instead, begin accepting yourself with all your flaws and imperfections, while also acknowledging and nurturing your natural gifts and good qualities. Remember, each moment presents an opportunity to cultivate the unique qualities of love within you and share them with others. By focusing your attention to these positive attributes, you will bring them onto your personal experience.

A simple yet powerful way to begin this journey is through affirmations that start with the words "I am," allowing you to connect not only with the qualities you already possess but also with those you wish to cultivate and nurture within yourself. For instance, you may say: *"I am loveable."* This can be more powerful if you look at yourself in a mirror, looking deeply into your eyes, and then repeating the positive affirmation loudly to yourself. Although it might be challenging at first to accept all that stands between you and the mirror, if you release all your self- judgement, gradually you will start to feel the love that wants to express itself through you.

As you say each affirmation, take a moment to feel it within you. Let it resonate in your heart and mind, allowing it to shape your thoughts, actions, and interactions. To help guide this practice, here are some positive qualities you can nurture within yourself through daily affirmations:

I am:

- *Calm*
- *Happy*
- *Grateful*
- *Forgivable*
- *Loving*
- *Loveable*
- *Compassionate*
- *Courageous*
- *Persistent*
- *Confident*
- *Wise*

- *Successful*
- *Kind*
- *Honest*
- *Generous*
- *Beautifull*
- *Creative*
- *Abundant*
- *Free*
- *Divine*

Repeat these words until they begin to feel true within you. Feel them resonate in every cell of your body, in every thought, in every breath. Know that the qualities you affirm are not just ideals to strive for - they are your true nature, waiting to be fully expressed. Remember, each time you speak them, you awaken the power, love, and light within you.

From Self-Acceptance to Divine Self-Expression

As you learn to accept yourself, and nurture your good qualities, you will begin to respect yourself more. With self-acceptance comes self-respect. This self-respect empowers you to set healthy boundaries, say "no" when needed, and to stand up for your rights. Self-respect naturally leads to self-care. You will begin to treasure your body by eating well, sleeping well, and exercising more, and you will act in a kind, gentle, and compassionate manner towards yourself.

Self-care flows into self-expression. You will begin to listen to your heart's voice. You will become clear of what you want, and how to live your life. You will find your true purpose and contribute your special gifts and talents for the benefits of humanity. Moreover, by uncovering your authenticity and appreciating your uniqueness, you will attract people who love you and respect you for who you really are. And finally, you will begin to see love everywhere around you, in each beautiful creation of the Universe, as you will realise that we are all one, and love is our Divine birthright.

Cultivating Forgiveness to Others

Q: Why is it important to forgive? And how can I forgive the people who hurt me in the past?

A: Forgiveness means letting go of the past. It is a conscious decision to release the negative feelings of anger, blame, resentment, or hate towards the people who have hurt you in the past. It is a process of letting go of those deeply held negative feelings within you. Forgiveness brings peace of mind and a sense of freedom from the pain you have suffered. Remember, only genuine forgiveness can help you heal completely and move forward in life.

Unforgiving people are consumed by doubts and fears, which distort their own perception of the reality. This is turn, interferes with their inner state of peace, and sense of calm. They are filled with sadness, or bitterness, and cannot see any light in the darkness in which they live. Those people live in despair, trapped in their own self-imposed pain and suffering, with little hope of release.

The reason for this self-created misery is the unwillingness of the unforgiving people to admit that each human being makes mistakes, and that mistakes should not be seen as "sins." "Sins" are only one's subjective interpretation of others' actions or behaviours, based on the limited beliefs about oneself, others, or the world. Thus, unforgiving people make decisions based on their subjective judgements about others' actions, and regard their personal judgements as absolutely true and irreversible.

It is important to understand that if left unexamined and unchallenged, a lack of forgiveness may interfere with your emotional, spiritual, and physical wellbeing. There is an old saying that says: *"Refusing to forgive someone is like drinking poison, and waiting for the other person to die."* By holding onto past hurts, you are the one suffering. Therefore, you need to forgive in order to heal yourself, reclaim your own joy, and your capacity to give and receive love.

Forgiveness is the First Step Towards Love

Forgiveness is often the first and most essential step towards truly loving yourself and others. As Mother Teresa said lovingly, *"If we really want to love, we must learn how to forgive."* When you hold on to anger or resentment, those feelings don't punish the person who hurt you - they quietly wound you from within. Hence, instead of allowing bitterness to poison your heart and your relationships, choose to cultivate deep understanding and genuine compassion for those who have wronged you in the past.

In order to forgive, you must first take responsibility for your own feelings. Those who refuse to do so, often fall into the trap of blaming others for their unhappiness. However, in this way, you hand over your power - seeing yourself as a victim of someone else's actions rather than the creator of your own peace.

The truth is that the past exists only in your mind. But each time you replay painful memories

- you relive them emotionally. By holding on to resentment, you keep yourself tied to suffering that no longer serves you. Forgiveness, on the other hand, frees your energy, softens your heart, and allows you to live fully in the present moment.

Forgiveness is a process - not a single act or decision. It unfolds gently as you begin to see both yourself and others through the eyes of compassion. The following steps can guide you through this inner journey, helping you release the pain, reclaim your peace, and open your heart to love again.

Steps to Forgive Those Who Hurt You

Here are some important steps for learning how to forgive others:

Step 1. Recognise the Impact: Acknowledge how your feelings of resentment affect your health, wellbeing, and emotional state in the present.

Step 2. Seek Understanding: Try to understand the reasons behind someone's actions. It is important to understand that generally, people do the best they can with the skills, knowledge, and awareness available to them at different stages of life. You may also reflect on some situations in your life when you personally needed forgiveness from another person. This can help you to empathise with the one who might need your forgiveness now.

Step 3. Affirm Forgiveness: To release yourself form the pain of your past events, you may also write and say loudly empowering affirmations for forgiveness. For example, you may repeat to yourself the following affirmations for forgiveness: *"I forgive those who have harmed me in my past, and I peacefully detach from them. I forgive them and I set them free."*

Step 4. Release Through Writing: One of the most powerful tools for cultivating forgiveness is the *"Forgiveness Letter."* This is a structured way to safely and consciously release your deeply ingrained negative feelings and reclaim your freedom. Importantly, this letter does not need to be sent to the person that hurt you - it is a very helpful tool for your own healing. Writing this letter can help you release the accumulated pain held in your body, mind, and soul, allowing you to begin healing from past hurts.

Forgiveness Letter

1. Prepare the Environment

Create a calm space free from interruptions. Allow yourself the time to fully engage with this practice. Remember, this is not a task to rush; healing is a process.

2. Write Your True Intention

Write longhand and begin with your intention:

My intention in writing this letter is to:

- *release any resentment or regret, and be free of the past;*

- *release any anger or hurt, so that I may move forward in peace and freedom.*

3. Express Your Thoughts and Feelings Honestly

Express all your thoughts and feelings towards the person you are holding anger, resentment, or other negative feelings against. Use "I felt..." statements to focus on your own past feelings and experiences, rather than blaming the other person. Please, be honest and specific about your feelings and thoughts. This is for your clarity and healing - it is not about confronting the other person.

1. *I felt angry that...*
2. *I felt afraid that...*
3. *I felt hurt that...*
4. *I felt sad that...*

4. Accept the Past and Move Forward

1. *I accept... (what happened)*
2. *I accept... (what is now)*
3. *The deep desire of my heart now is...*
4. *What I am doing to support myself now is...*

5. Engage with the Universe

1. *What I am asking from the Universe now is...*
2. *My loving and powerful intention in moving forward is...*

To illustrate how this process works in practice, here is an example from my counselling practice.

Matthew, a marketing manager in his late thirties, came to counselling deeply upset after a colleague, Robert, had publicly criticised him during a team meeting. The incident left him feeling humiliated and betrayed. Although months had passed, the anger still lived inside him - tightening his chest each time he thought about it. Using the *"Forgiveness Letter"*, he wrote:

"My intention in writing this letter is to release my anger towards Robert and to reclaim my peace and self-confidence. I no longer want this resentment to live inside me. I want to be free, calm, and able to move forward with peace, clarity, and strength.

I felt angry that Robert criticised me unfairly, especially in front of others. His words cut deeply because they weren't true, yet they lingered in the air and made me feel small. I felt angry that I wasn't given a chance to explain myself, that my efforts and integrity were dismissed in a single moment. That anger has lived in me since then - a quiet flame that I can now see has only burned me, not him.

I felt afraid that I would never be respected in my workplace again. His criticism made me doubt myself - my competence, my value, even my right to belong where I am. I started second-guessing every decision, wondering how others saw me. That fear took away my joy in work, replacing it with constant tension. Today, I choose to let that fear go. I know that my worth isn't determined by anyone's opinion of me.

I felt hurt that someone I trusted could betray me. We had worked closely together - shared ideas, challenges, even laughter. I never expected that Robert would turn against me in that way. The hurt came not only from what he said but from the breaking of that trust. It made me question whether kindness and openness were safe. Now, I can see that his actions spoke more about his own pain and insecurity than about who I am. I no longer want to carry the weight of his choices.

I felt sad that our professional relationship ended in conflict. I had hoped we could work as a team, supporting each other towards common goals. The loss of that connection saddened me because it represented not just a disagreement, but the end of mutual respect. Even so, I honour what that relationship once was and the lessons it has brought me.

I accept that this event happened and that I cannot change the past. I accept that I can control only my response, not the actions of others. Holding on to anger has not protected me - it has only kept me bound to the past. I release the need to be right or to be vindicated. I release the story that I must be perfect to be respected.

The deep desire of my heart now is to feel peace and joy in my work. I want to walk into each day with confidence, unburdened by old wounds. What I'm doing to support myself now is focusing on my strengths, setting healthy boundaries, and surrounding myself with colleagues who uplift and inspire me. I am learning to speak my truth calmly, to trust my abilities, and to protect my inner peace.

What I am asking from the Universe now is clarity and confidence - clarity to see every situation with wisdom and understanding, and confidence to stay grounded in my worth. I am grateful that this experience, as painful as it was, has taught me resilience, self-awareness, and compassion. It has shown me that forgiveness is not weakness; it is strength.

My loving and powerful intention in moving forward is to maintain peace in all relationships and to act with integrity and kindness, no matter what others choose. I now release Robert with empathy and understanding, and I release myself from this story. I am free."

After completing the letter, Matthew reported feeling an immediate sense of relief, as if a heavy weight had lifted. Over time, his stress reduced, his energy increased, and he experienced a renewed ability to engage with others from a place of calm, love, and confidence.

The Transformative Power of Forgiveness

Remember, forgiveness is a gift to yourself. It releases the grip of the past, allowing you to live fully in the present. By forgiving, you reclaim your own power, restore your inner harmony, and open your heart to love and connection.

True forgiveness is a bridge to compassion, understanding, and joy. When you forgive, you also reconnect with the source of love within yourself. Then, you will realise that love is not conditional, that every human being is deserving of compassion and understanding, and that you are inherently worthy of peace and happiness.

Forgiveness is not just an act of the mind - it is a profound transformation of the heart. It frees your spirit, restores your energy, and allows your life to flow with greater abundance, creativity, and connection. By practising forgiveness, you align yourself with the divine rhythm of life - a life in which love, peace, and freedom are your natural inheritance.

Self-Forgiveness

"You are not guilty of any sin, my brother. But you believe that you are. And while you believe this, you will need forgiveness. It is the only way out of your self-imposed illusion."
-Paul Ferrini ("Love Without Conditions")

Q: How do I forgive myself for my wrong actions in the past?

A: Self-forgiveness is one of the most profound acts of liberation you can offer to yourself. It is the key to freeing your heart from the heavy chains of shame and guilt that silently drain your energy, peace, and joy. When you refuse to forgive yourself, unknowingly, you perpetuate the same emotional wounds that once hurt you. Therefore, you may continue to harm others and yourself in the same way you have been harmed in the past.

Self-forgiveness, however, opens the door to healing and transformation. It dissolves the toxic energy of guilt and reconnects you with your true essence - the part of you that has always been worthy of love. As you release those burdens, you will begin to see yourself more clearly, and you will relate to others with greater compassion and authenticity.

One powerful example of the transformative power of self-forgiveness is the story of Clara, a 42-year-old woman who came to me consumed by resentment and bitterness after her divorce. Her former husband, Adam had remarried happily, and although Clara outwardly pretended to have moved on, deep inside she felt humiliated, unworthy, and betrayed.

When photos of Adam's new life appeared on social media - radiant smiles, holidays, celebrations - a rush of anger surged through her. *"It's not fair. He gets to be happy while I'm left in pieces,"* she confessed. In moments of bitterness, Clara began sharing exaggerated and sometimes false stories about Adam's behaviour during their marriage. She insinuated to mutual acquaintances that he had married for money or convenience, casting doubt on the authenticity of his new life.

"It made me feel powerful for a moment... like I could still hurt him the way he hurt me." she

said later. Yet the relief was fleeting. Each time she gossiped or saw the discomfort on a friend's face, shame crept in. At night, guilt whispered in her mind: *"What are you becoming?"* She felt trapped between her unresolved anger and her conscience - unable to stop, yet unable to find peace.

Over time, Clara noticed that her bitterness had begun to spill into other areas of her life. She grew impatient with her teenage daughter, distant from her close friends, and emotionally numb at work. *"I couldn't recognise myself anymore,"* she said to me quietly. *"I thought I was defending my dignity, but I was really destroying it."*

Through our sessions, Clara began to uncover the deeper truth beneath her anger. Her actions had not come from cruelty or malice, but from an unhealed wound - the pain of feeling unworthy and unloved. She realised that spreading rumours was her unconscious way of crying out, *"See my pain. You have to acknowledge that I mattered."*

Gradually, she learned to separate her behaviour from her essence. She reflected, *"I wasn't born bitter or vindictive. I became that way because I didn't know how to heal myself. That's why I was hurting others."* This insight became her turning point. With gentle guidance, she began to forgive herself. In the course of time, she wrote a letter to her wounded heart: *"I forgive you, Clara, for letting your pain speak louder than the truth. I see now that your anger was really grief, and your gossip was your way of trying to hold onto your ego. I understand now that you were trying to protect yourself - your unbearable sadness. I release the guilt I've held for the harm my actions caused. I choose to learn from this mistake and open my heart to love again - beginning with myself."*

As she read the letter aloud, tears streamed down her face. Something within her softened. For the first time in years, she felt compassion for the woman she had been for years - lost, rejected, and longing to be seen. In the weeks that followed, Clara found herself speaking of her ex-husband with neutrality, even kindness. *"For the first time in years, I don't feel the need to tear him down anymore,"* she said one day with a quiet smile. *"I just want to be free."*

Clara's healing went even further. She reached out to Adam and his wife, expressing her sincere apologies for any pain she had caused and asking for their forgiveness. This courageous step brought her a profound sense of closure and inner freedom. She realised that forgiveness - both of herself and by others - was a gift that unburdened her heart and opened the door to love again.

Clara's journey reminds us that self-forgiveness does not excuse past harmful behaviour - it transforms it. It helps us understand the roots of our pain, reclaim the wisdom it carries, and reopen our hearts to love again.

The Path to Self-Forgiveness

Although it might seem difficult to forgive yourself for the harm you have caused to others, several effective steps can guide you through this process. To begin the self-forgiving process, you need to look back on any of these experiences in the past that continue to evoke guilt or shame.

Look deeply into your motivations at the time - not to justify your actions, but to understand them. If you do this, you might discover that your deepest intention was to protect yourself or meet some of your needs in the best possible way you knew at that moment. Remember, you acted with the level of awareness, strength, and emotional maturity you had then. You may have lacked another perspective or self-control, but you were doing your best within your limitations as a human being.

Being human means making mistakes. Making mistakes is part of life's learning process. In fact, in the process of learning there are no mistakes, there are only learning opportunities. You need to accept your limitations, let go of your perfectionist aspirations, and honour your humanity. When you embrace your imperfections with compassion, guilt transforms into wisdom, and self-condemnation gives way to self-understanding. This is the essence of true healing - to love yourself not despite your flaws, but through them.

To forgive yourself completely, you also need to nurture self-compassion. In her amazing book, *"Self-Compassion,"* Kristin Neff explains: *"Self-compassion honours the fact that all human beings are fallible, that wrong choices and feelings of regret are inevitable..."* The reality is that each human being has harmed at least one other person in their life. Like many other human beings, you acted in ways that harmed someone else. However, when you carefully examine your mistakes in the past, it becomes clear that you did not consciously decide to make them. Even in some rare cases when you did make a conscious choice, you may realise that the intention behind your actions was coloured by your past limiting beliefs or previous traumatic experiences. Knowing this truth can help you to have more compassion for yourself, and forgive yourself completely. It is time to let go of the burden of the past.

From my experience, many people struggle with lingering guilt that keeps them emotionally stuck. If you'd like to understand this feeling more deeply and discover ways to free yourself from it, you will find a detailed exploration in the third book of my trilogy, "*Another Way of Living: How to Dissolve the Ego and Realise Your Divine Potential*", especially in the chapter *"Guilt and Release from It."* Here is a genuine testimonial from one of my readers from Australia, Macari Barin, about this chapter: *"I wish I learned Lesson 13 "Guilt and Release from It" from your amazing book "Another Way of Living: How to Dissolve the Ego and Realise Your Divine Potential" 20 years ago. It would have saved so many years of insanity and darkness. Thank you for your wisdom. You truly are one of a kind, and God willing, the light that can light all of our candles."*

If you still resist forgiving yourself for your past actions, you may give a sincere, meaningful, and heartfelt apology to those you have harmed in the past. You may let them know that you did not hurt them intentionally, and that you will treat them with respect in the future. When you offer a heartfelt apology to those you have hurt, you show them that you truly care about their feelings. Therefore, if you take the courage to admit your mistakes, you will develop a deep sense of respect from others. Moreover, when you have the courage to acknowledge your mistakes, you will develop a strong sense of self-respect. This self-respect will in turn, improve your self-esteem, and your overall life satisfaction.

To overcome the overwhelming feelings of shame and guilt, some people may wish to reach out to a Higher Power, to something greater than our individual selves. Regardless of your spiritual beliefs, a prayer to God, or asking the Universe for forgiveness, coupled with a promise to act differently next time, can powerfully support the process of self-forgiveness.

Most importantly, as you cultivate this practice of self-forgiveness, you gradually open the door to inner peace, allowing your spirit to breathe freely once more. The heavy clouds of shame and regret will lift, revealing the boundless potential that has always been yours. When you forgive yourself completely for your past mistakes, you will align with a higher, more loving source of energy. Hence, you will become more loving, more compassionate, and more understanding towards yourself and others. Self-forgiveness will transform your inner world, turning pain into wisdom and separation into love. Then, you will know that joy and light are not found outside of you - they have always been within, waiting to shine through your every word, action, and breath.

Developing Compassion

"The greatest degree of inner tranquility comes from the development of love and compassion. The more we care for the happiness of others, the greater our own sense of wellbeing becomes."
- Dalai Lama

Q: How do people develop compassion?

A: Compassion is the highest form of love expressed towards another human being. It literally means "to suffer together," so you feel motivated to help the other person to relieve that suffering. In compassion, the wellbeing of another human being becomes more important than your own. Compassion has a profound healing power when the person who suffers is shown unconditional love, care, and acceptance. In fact, authentic, deep compassion can transform, and even heal the person who suffers.

Compassion can be developed when you are faced with the greatest challenges in life. In those challenging situations, the people who disturb you the most, can actually offer you a precious opportunity to grow your compassionate heart. Those people offer you a challenge, and by trying to overcome that challenge peacefully, you can learn true compassion. In this way, the people who have made you feel uneasy, can, paradoxically, become your best teachers.

This truth became clear in the story of Barbara, a client who came to me feeling utterly drained by her colleague, Diana, who seemed determined to undermine her. *"I feel like she's constantly trying to make me look incompetent,"* Barbara confessed, her voice tight with tension. *"No matter what I do, it's never good enough. I feel embarrassed, humiliated, and angry."*

At first, Barbara couldn't see beyond her frustration. She was caught in a cycle of defensiveness and self-doubt, questioning her worth and replaying every unpleasant encounter in her mind. *"I can't stop thinking about what Diana said all day,"* she admitted. *"It's like a constant replay in my mind - every tone, every glance. I'm exhausted."* Early on, Barbara's instinct was to fight back - through sarcasm, sharp replies, or silent withdrawal. Yet each reaction only deepened her sense of disconnection and inner conflict. The more she resisted, the more power Diana's behaviour seemed to have over her.

It was in our counselling sessions that this pattern slowly came into focus. Barbara began to explore not only her emotions but also the subtle human dynamics behind them. *"Why does she trigger me so much?"* she asked one day, her voice trembling with curiosity rather than anger for the first time. That question opened a doorway to empathy - not condoning Diana's behaviour but seeking to understand it.

As Barbara reflected, she began to recognise the behavioural triggers that shaped Diana's interactions. Diana often spoke harshly during stressful periods - after tense phone calls, before project deadlines, or when upper management was present. There were moments, too, when Diana seemed distracted, staring blankly at her computer screen as if her thoughts were far away.

She slowly learned that Diana's life outside the office was not as composed as she appeared. Diana was going through a painful divorce, caring for an elderly parent, and struggling to meet her own performance targets. This realisation didn't excuse her behaviour, but it humanised her. *"I never thought about that,"* Barbara said softly. *"Maybe it's not about me. Maybe she's just trying to keep herself from falling apart."*

Through counselling, Barbara began exploring her feelings more deeply. She started to consider that her colleague's behaviour might reflect not Barbara's shortcomings, but her own stress, insecurity, and even personal struggles at home. *"I hadn't considered that,"* Barbara said slowly. *"I guess she's had a lot going on outside of work too... maybe that's why she's so harsh sometimes."*

This shift in her perception marked a turning point. Barbara began practising small, conscious changes in how she responded. The next time Diana criticised her work in a meeting, Barbara paused, took a slow breath, and said, *"Thank you for your feedback, I'll take that into consideration."* For the first time, she felt a subtle sense of power - not the power to dominate, but the power to remain centred. *"I can't believe it,"* she told me afterward. *"I didn't explode, and I didn't feel crushed. I just... stayed calm and present."*

As the weeks went by, Barbara's emotional landscape began to shift. She started noticing details she had missed before - the tremor in Diana's voice, the tension in her shoulders, the quiet sighs between her sentences. Beneath the hostility, there was weariness, fear, and loneliness.

Instead of reacting with anger, Barbara began responding with compassion. She started offering small gestures - a warm greeting, a genuine "thank you," or a simple acknowledgment of Diana's effort during a meeting. These weren't strategic moves; they were sincere expressions of understanding.

To her surprise, Diana's tone gradually softened. There were still moments of tension, but the energy between them began to change. One morning, Diana quietly thanked Barbara for staying late to help her finish a report - something Barbara never expected to hear. *"I never thought I could see her like this,"* Barbara reflected. *"I used to want to prove her wrong. Now, I just... understand her. And that makes me feel lighter, calmer. It's like I've stopped fighting a war inside myself."*

Barbara's transformation didn't just improve her workplace experience; it deepened her relationship with herself. She no longer needed external validation to feel secure. She realised that true strength comes from compassion - not only for others but also for one's own pain and vulnerability. *"I feel more in control of my emotions, more peaceful,"* she said during our final session. *"It's as if a heavy curtain has lifted. I can see more clearly now - both her struggles and my own. And that understanding brings freedom."*

What Barbara discovered on a personal level reflects a universal lesson - one that extends far beyond individual relationships. In this modern age, we all need to cultivate inner peace, non-violence, and compassion. History reminds us that these qualities have the power to heal not only hearts but nations. Nelson Mandela, who endured 27 years in prison under harsh conditions, could have harboured anger and resentment towards those who imprisoned him. Instead, he chose compassion and understanding. He empathised with his former oppressors, reached out to build bridges, and worked towards reconciliation and nation-building in South Africa. Mandela's ability to transform personal suffering into understanding and care for others demonstrates that compassion is not just a private virtue - it can reshape history.

Mother Teresa devoted her life to serving the poorest and most marginalised people in India, offering them love, care, and dignity. Mahatma Gandhi chose non-violence and forgiveness as tools for social change, emphasising compassion and understanding even towards his opponents.

We also need to promote these good human values among others. Compassion, patience, and understanding are not just personal virtues - they are the invisible threads that hold our families, communities, and even nations together. When we live these values openly, we become quiet examples of what it means to live with awareness and heart.

True compassion begins within, but it expands far beyond ourselves. Every act of patience, every moment of understanding, sends a ripple outward, touching lives we may never even know. By nurturing it in our hearts and reflecting it in our actions, we help build a more peaceful, humane world. As Dalai Lama emphasised: *The cultivation of compassion is no longer a luxury, but a necessity, if our species is to survive.*

Cultivating Compassion in Your Daily Life

Compassion is a conscious choice. In challenging situations, you can either engage with the good qualities of love, empathy, and consideration of others, or allow anger, sadness, jealousy or hatred to take over. If you choose the latter, you will discover that your real enemies are not the people who challenge you, but your own fear, anger, and resentment. Those negative feelings are the antidotes of compassion and therefore, you need to find a way to transcend them.

To cultivate compassion, it is important to remember that every human being is seeking happiness. Every human being has a right to overcome their own suffering and simply be happy. If you truly understand this, you will automatically feel an increased level of sensitivity, love, closeness, and compassion for others. And yet, the ability to extend this compassion outward begins within.

To truly feel compassion for others, you must first cultivate self-compassion. When you nurture a mental state of inner peace and boundless love within yourself, your understanding of others deepens naturally. You begin to act with greater patience, kindness, and generosity.

From this expanded awareness, gentle questions may arise: *"What can I do to help those around me?"* or *"How can I contribute to the happiness of others and the society as a whole?"* Even small acts inspired by these reflections can make a meaningful difference in the world. Remember, ultimately you are serving humanity, and serving humanity is the ultimate purpose, and the greatest achievement in life. Serving and helping the humanity will shift your focus beyond yourself. It will give you a sense that there are worthwhile things greater than yourself.

When you open your heart with genuine compassion, you become a source of light -not just for yourself, but for all who cross your path. Compassion allows you to rise above self-interest, to see the shared humanity in every soul, and to act in ways that heal, uplift, and inspire. By embracing compassion fully - in your thoughts, words, and deeds - you awaken a deep, transformative power within, creating a life rich with joy, purpose, and connection for yourself and those around you.

Let your heart be the compass of your life. Choose compassion in every moment, and you will not only transform the world around you but also awaken the boundless love and light that have always lived within you.

Exploring the Meaning of Human Life

"Life is the gift; the unspeakable treasure; the holy of the holies."
- Neale Donald Walsh

Q: What is the meaning of human life?

A: Life has no inherent meaning on its own. You are the only one who gives it meaning. Therefore, your main purpose in life is to realise who you really are, and then consciously determine who you want to become.

The reality is that many people live unconsciously, carried by the flow of circumstances, shaped by their past experiences, and influenced by others' expectations. However, you need to understand that in order to change your current undesirable conditions, you must first accept the responsibility for creating them - even if you did so unconsciously. Only then can you choose to transform those unwanted conditions and use your life to create the person you have always wanted to be. This transformation may require changing certain aspects of your life that no longer reflect the vision of the self you wish to express in the world. And as you move through this process, it is essential to bless both your past and your present, for every experience has led you to this moment of awakening. From here, you can aspire for your highest self-creation.

You can learn to become the creator of your experiences by consciously choosing thoughts that align with what you want to bring into your life each day. This is the essence of conscious living. Every thought and every spoken word carries a powerful vibrational imprint. At the deepest level, each thought, decision, and action arises from one of two sources - love or fear - and only you can choose which one to follow. It is important to remember that your thoughts determine your feelings, and your feelings shape your life experiences. When you send out energy rooted in fear, you attract fear-based situations. Yet at any moment, you can choose differently. Remember, through your thoughts, words, and deeds, you are continually re-creating your life.

Each moment offers an opportunity to decide who you wish to become by acting in alignment with what you feel passionate about. Every time you choose love over fear and follow your passion, you reconnect with a deeper truth of who you are. Passion is the driving force behind your highest self-expression. Without it, life becomes flat, empty, and disconnected. With it, life becomes meaningful, vibrant, and filled with purpose. Ultimately, the true purpose of life is to discover your passion, embody the highest version of yourself, and live fully - with joy, authenticity, and love.

The truth is that each human being carries some special talent - a gift, a hidden treasure within. In her timeless book *"The Game of Life and How to Play it,"* Florence Scovel Shinn wrote, *"There is for each man, perfect self-expression. There is a place which he is to fill and no one else can fill, something which he is to do, which no one else can do, it is his destiny!"*

It takes great courage to be truthful with yourself and to listen to your heart. Yet if you lack the courage to follow your heart, your joy will slowly wither, and a part of you will begin to die. But the moment you find the strength to trust your heart and walk its path, you will go into the unknown, despite all your fears. By listening to the inner call of your heart and following its guidance, you will always move in the right direction in life. Each step into the unknown will bring a deeper sense of freedom and joy, and you will feel truly alive. By answering the quiet call of your heart, you will uncover the limitless possibilities that life holds for you - and in doing so, you will see all your dreams come true.

Many people spend years searching for the right path that feels truly aligned with who they are. If you are uncertain about your true purpose or ideal vocation, and if you feel inspired to explore your own path more deeply, I have included insightful guidance and a specially designed, research-based test in my second book of the trilogy, *"Another Way of Living: A Journey to Self-Realisation (Book 2)"*. This tool is created to help you discover the right career path that aligns with your passions and your natural strengths and talents. Over the years, I have seen how profoundly this clinically proven career test has helped my clients find clarity and confidence in their life direction. Many of them now lead deeply fulfilling and purpose-driven lives.

One of the most inspiring examples is Larissa's story. When she first came to me at nineteen, she felt adrift and uninspired in her work as a gardener - trapped in a routine that felt painfully disconnected from her true self. Each morning, as she tended to the plants and flowers around her, she couldn't shake the emptiness growing inside. *"I feel like I'm withering while everything else around me blooms,"* she once confessed softly. Though she loved nature, she sensed that her life was meant for something more - something that stirred her soul.

Beneath her quiet exterior was a deep longing for expression, creativity, and meaning. Yet fear and self-doubt held her back. She often questioned herself: *"What if I'm not talented enough? What if I fail?"* Like many young people, she had internalised the belief that following her passion was risky, unrealistic, or even selfish.

Through counselling, and after completing the research-based career test mentioned earlier, Larissa began to see herself more clearly. The results revealed her natural artistic inclination, strong auditory sensitivity, and creative imagination - all pointing unmistakably towards music. For the first time, she felt a spark of recognition, as if a long-forgotten truth was returning to her awareness.

With growing courage, Larissa decided to follow her heart. She began experimenting with DJing and composing her own music in her small bedroom studio. Slowly, the melodies she created became her language of freedom and joy. Within a short time, her talent was noticed, and she was offered a contract with one of the world's leading DJ companies. She quit her full-time job as a gardener and devoted herself entirely to music.

Today, Larissa lives solely through her music, travelling internationally and performing for audiences across the globe. Her art now brings joy not only to her own heart but to thousands of people who dance to her music and feel her passion through every beat. She often says that discovering her passion for music didn't just change her career - it gave her back her sense of self. She feels authentic, joyful, and fulfilled. Larissa's story reminds us that when we dare to listen to our inner voice and act with courage, life responds in extraordinary ways.

The truth is that only you can decide who you wish to become in this world. This journey starts by quieting your mind and allowing your inner world to reveal a clear vision of your highest self-expression. In this process, go as deep as you can - beneath the noise of your thoughts, beneath the layers of fear - until you reach the still place where your soul begins to whisper its truth. From that sacred space, imagine yourself as the most radiant, magnificent version of yourself. As you hold that vision, begin gently transforming your limiting beliefs into empowering ones that resonate with the grandest image of yourself.

Remember that you can be, do, and have anything your heart truly desires. You have the freedom to choose the places, the people, the circumstances, even the challenges that will help you grow into your highest potential. Along the way, don't forget to feel grateful for each person and each situation you encounter, knowing that everything in life is happening with a reason. Through right thinking and conscious living, you can create a life overflowing with joy, abundance, and fulfillment - a life that reflects the beauty and truth of who you truly are.

To bring this wisdom into your daily life, try the following practical exercise:

Practical Exercise: Discovering and Living Your Highest Self

This simple yet powerful exercise will help you to connect with your passion, align with your highest self, and begin taking conscious steps towards a more meaningful, purpose-driven life.

Step 1: Find Time for Quiet Reflection

- Find a quiet place where you won't be disturbed. Close your eyes, take a few deep breaths, and allow your mind to settle.

- Then, ask yourself silently: *"What brings me the deepest joy? What makes me feel fully alive?"*

- Please, don't censor your answers. Write down whatever comes to your mind, even if it feels impossible or unexpected.

Step 2: Identify Your Passion

- Review your list and circle the activities or interests that excite you the most.

- Now ask yourself: *"If I could spend more time doing this, how would I feel?"*

- Stay with these feelings as long as possible. Let their warmth and vitality expand through your entire Being.

Step 3: Visualise Your Highest Self

- Close your eyes again and imagine yourself five years from now, living as the fullest expression of your true self.

- See where you are, what you are doing, who is with you, and how you feel.

- Let this vision be vivid and alive - feel the joy, freedom, and sense of purpose flowing through your entire body and soul.

Step 4: Transform Your Limiting Beliefs

- Write down the beliefs that may be holding you back (for example, *"I am too old," "I'm not good enough,"* or *"It's too late for me"*).

- Next to each limiting belief, write a new empowering belief, such as, *"It is never too late to pursue my passion," "I am worthy of success, abundance, and joy," "Each step I take aligns me with my destiny."*

Step 5: Take One Inspired Action

- Choose one small action you can take this week that will help you move closer to your vision.

- It might be signing up for a class, reaching out to a mentor, practising your craft, or simply dedicating time each day to nurture your passion.

Step 6: Connect with Your Highest Self Each Day

- Start your day with a short ritual: take a few deep breaths, close your eyes, and connect with your highest self.

- Ask yourself: *"What choice can I make today that brings me closer to the highest version of myself?"* Allow this question to guide your thoughts, words, and actions throughout the day.

- Throughout the day, pause whenever you notice stress, doubt, or distraction. Ask yourself: *"Is this thought, word, or action serving my highest self?"*

- Make small, conscious adjustments as needed - whether it's speaking with kindness, dedicating time to your passion, or choosing love over fear.

- End your day with reflection: note one way you lived aligned with your highest self and one area to improve tomorrow.

Remember, real transformation rarely happens

overnight. It blossoms gently through each conscious choice you make to honour your truth and follow your heart. Each moment you choose love over fear and courage over doubt, you step closer to a life illuminated with meaning, fulfillment, and joy.

Achieving Self-Realisation

"If you would live according to the natural law, you would have all the freedom, all the joy, all the peace, and all the wisdom, understanding and power of the Spirit you are. You would be a fully realised being."
- Neale Donald Walsch

Q: What is self-realisation and how can we achieve it?

A: In truth, all the peace, love, and happiness you seek, is not outside of you, but within you - in the very essence of your Being. To experience and permanently live in this state of infinite peace, boundless joy, and unconditional love is what self-realisation is all about.

For many people, it is difficult to imagine a state of complete inner calm, free from the usual turbulence of thoughts, feelings, or constant activity. This is because most of us are conditioned to perceive the world primarily through the narrow lens of the five senses. We are constantly aware of everything happening around us, yet often unaware of our own existence, of our own Being. In this way, our true self remains unknown to ourselves.

Yet beneath that noise, there is a still, silent presence - our Being - our true nature. Unless we come to know ourselves directly, we can never truly understand ourselves or others, and we will remain in ignorance. Unless we become aware of our own Being, discover our essence, and reach self-realisation, we will continue to live in fear, misery, and suffering. Notably, we will not only be afraid of others, but we will be afraid of ourselves, because we won't know who we truly are.

It is essential to realise that you cannot experience true joy without knowing your true self. How can you be peaceful and joyous if you don't know who you really are? To begin answering the deeper question of your existence, you must dive into the silence - beyond the noise of the mind - and uncover the truth within.

When you reach self-realisation, you will experience a joy greater than any worldly pleasure, a freedom beyond anything the world can offer. You will feel as though you have been born anew. You will live aligned with your true essence - no longer bound by the false image created by the ego, but radiant, free, and authentic. As one of my clients, Chris, a 55-year-old businessman, expressed after years of chasing happiness only through wealth and success: *"When I finally touched that quiet presence within me, I realised that I already had everything I was chasing outside. For the first time in my life, I felt complete."*

The more you get to know your true self, the more loving you will naturally become. The more loving you become, the more you will begin to live in the present moment. And the more you live in the present, the more alive you will feel. Then, every action, no matter how small, will be done with your total presence. As a result, your life will become a blissful experience.

Remember that the more you are aware of your own Being, the more you can become. And the more you become, the more yet you can be. As Paramhansa Yogananda wrote: *"The deeper the self-realisation of a man, the more he influences the whole Universe by his subtle spiritual vibrations, and the less he himself is affected by the phenomenal flux."* Therefore, your most important task in life is to make space among your daily activities, get in touch with your inner Being, and reach self-realisation.

Connecting deeply with your inner self is both a practice and a gift - a journey of discovery that allows you to meet the truest, most authentic part of who you are. One of the most powerful ways to cultivate this connection is through meditation. You can begin simply, dedicating just five to ten minutes twice a day - once in the morning to set the tone for your day, and once in the evening to gently release the events of the day. During these sessions, focus your attention on the natural rhythm of your breath, observing it without judgement, and allow yourself to become aware of the calm and stillness that already resides within you, patiently waiting to be recognised.

As this practice becomes more familiar and effortless, gradually extend each meditation session to around thirty minutes. Over time, once you feel comfortable with these dedicated periods, begin to carry that sense of meditative awareness into your daily life. Allow the steady, gentle calm you cultivate during meditation to flow through every action, every thought, and every interaction, transforming ordinary moments into opportunities for presence, clarity, and serenity. Whenever possible, after your meditation, remain seated in silent reflection, soaking in that peaceful state of mind. This is when the deepest enjoyment and the most profound benefits of meditation naturally arise.

By nurturing this stillness regularly, you will find that your inner calm extends beyond your formal practice, gradually permeating your daily life. When your mind quiets, you may gently pose to yourself the timeless question: *"Who am I?"* Hold this question as a companion without expecting a ready-made answer shaped by past beliefs, habits, or assumptions. When you least anticipate it, the answer will emerge from the deepest recesses of your Being, revealing the truth of your existence. As Sogyal Rinpoche proclaimed, *"It is meditation that slowly purifies the ordinary mind, unmasking and exhausting its habits and illusions, so that we can, at the right moment, recognise who we really are."*

Among the many meditative techniques I have personally used, one in particular has been profoundly transformative for me. This guided meditation technique has helped me to awaken the light, peace, and joy within, and has been a cornerstone in my own path towards self-realisation. I want to share it with you so that you may experience the same inner connection. You can also find a full guided version of this meditation technique on my YouTube channel, *Dr Snezhana*, titled *"Awaken Your Inner Light with Dr Snezhana."* This meditation is designed to help you connect deeply with your higher self - the source of your intuition, inner wisdom, and limitless creativity. With regular practice, it will bring serenity, clarity, and deep spiritual connection to your inner self.

Here is a brief outline of this meditation technique to get you started:

Meditation Technique: Awaken Your Inner Light

• Find a Quiet Space

Choose a peaceful place where you won't be disturbed. Sit comfortably with your spine upright and relaxed. Let your chest open, your shoulders soften, and your hands rest gently, palms facing upward on your thighs. Feel yourself becoming still and present. Allow the outer world to fade into silence as you turn inward.

- ## **Focus on Your Breath**

Begin by exhaling through your mouth in two short breaths - releasing tension and old energy. Inhale deeply through your nose, hold for a gentle count of four, then exhale through your open mouth in two short breaths. The purpose of exhaling through an open mouth is to help release carbon dioxide from your lungs, promoting a sense of cleansing and relaxation throughout your body.

Repeat this rhythmic cycle three times, allowing each breath to draw you deeper into calmness. With every exhalation, feel your body relax; with every inhalation, feel your awareness brighten.

- ## **Focus on the Inner Light**

Now, gently turn your eyes slightly upward, directing your inner gaze towards the point between your eyebrows - the spiritual centre of concentration, known as the third eye. Fix your attention lightly there, without strain.

Imagine a soft, radiant glow emerging within your heart - a warm light of peace and joy. Allow this gentle light to expand, first filling your chest, then your entire body. Feel it radiating outward - into your surroundings, your home, your loved ones, your community, your country, and ultimately, into the vast expanse of the Universe. Merge completely with this luminous presence, becoming one with the infinite ocean of light.

- **Affirm Your True Nature**

When your heart feels open and peaceful, silently repeat these affirmations, letting each one resonate through your entire Being:

- *I release all burdens.*
- *I open myself to Divine love, peace, and wisdom.*
- *I am not the body.*
- *I am not the mind.*
- *I am the eternal sphere of light and joy.*
- *I am peace.*
- *I am love.*
- *I am joy.*
- *I am bliss.*

Feel these words not just as thoughts, but as living truths awakening within you.

- **Completion**

To complete your meditation, exhale gently in three double breaths. Offer your gratitude - to the Universe, to your higher self, and to the Divine presence within you. When you are ready, slowly open your eyes, carrying the calm, light, and stillness of your meditation into the world around you.

- **Integration**

Carry this light, joy, and peace into your daily life. Let it guide your thoughts, words, and actions.

Through this meditation practice, you will awaken a profound sense of wholeness, freedom, and Divine presence. It is a sacred pathway that will help you align with your higher self, radiating love and light into the world. By nurturing this daily connection, you will begin to live fully in the present, guided by your inner wisdom, and illuminated by your eternal light.

Remember, self-realisation is not a distant goal to be reached - it is your true essence - quietly waiting to be recognised. The more you honour this truth, the more your life unfolds as a living expression of peace, love, and Divine grace.

Uniting

My heart wanted to talk to yours...
Are you free? I've just wanted to...
Well, I am feeling so warm, and so complete,
so happy...
Can I just be next to you?
This stream of joy is unstoppable,
No way can it come to a halt.
It must find its way down the hill,
Through the valley,
Among the trees and bushes,
Before it reaches the bigger brother.
The bigger brother is Him,
So, we become one
In our pursuit for eternity...

Let's Share the Light

"From the depths of my heart, I thank you for reading this book. If even a single page has brought you clarity, comfort, or inspiration, I invite you to share your experience with others. Your voice can make a difference. By leaving a short review on Amazon or any other global book platform, you may inspire someone else to take their first step on a journey toward inner peace, immense joy, and true freedom. Your words could be the spark that lights the way for another person to transform their life.

Helping others to feel better also nurtures your own happiness - every act of kindness and sharing sends ripples of light into the world. When we uplift one another, we make the world brighter, more loving, and more compassionate for all.

*I would also love to hear from you personally - what touched you, what inspired you, or what questions arose in your heart while reading. You can always reach me at **hello@ anotherwayeducation.org**, or by leaving* a video message or question on my YouTube channel, **Dr Snezhana**, where over 30,000 people from across the globe gather for inspiration and encouragement. I welcome your questions with love and will be delighted to offer personal guidance and words of support. This is our chance to connect - heart to heart, soul to soul.

If this book has made a difference in your life, I warmly invite you to share it with someone you care about. A friend, a colleague, a family member - perhaps someone quietly struggling to find their peace. Often, the right message at the right moment can change the entire course of someone's life.

And because I want this exciting journey together to extend beyond these pages, I am offering a **FREE introductory counselling or coaching session inspired by the wisdom of this book.** These sessions are designed to uplift, to provide practical tools, and to remind you of the strength and beauty that already exist within you. If you, or someone you love, would benefit, simply send me an email at **hello@anotherwayeducation. org,** and I will gladly arrange a time that works for both of us. This offering comes from my heart - no fees, no obligations - only pure love. Together, *let us keep spreading light. The more we share peace, compassion, and joy, the brighter this world becomes.*

May your awakened light shine in every thought, word, and deed, illuminating your path and inspiring all who encounter your presence."

With love and blessing,

Snezhana Djambazova-Popordanoska